Disney

VILLAINS

Devilishly Delicious Cookbook

VILLAINS

Devilishly Delicious Cookbook

Julie Tremaine

INSIGHT
EDITIONS

San Rafael · Los Angeles · London

Contents

Main Courses

Cakes & Pies

Drinks

Cookies & Sweets

Introduction

For decades, the Disney Villains have been scheming and plotting, entertaining us with their dastardly ways. From Chernabog's long, dark shadow to Maleficent's curse, the Disney Villains show us how to embrace our evil side and have some fun along the way.

In this cookbook, you will find recipes for delicious appetizers, entrées, desserts, drinks, and more—all inspired by the iconic villains from Disney's beloved film library. Wickedly good dishes like baked Poison Apples, Magic Flower Salad, and Unbirthday Cake are wickedly outstanding treats for your next Disney Villains-themed party, Halloween bash, or fun family night. Conjuring a tasty dish or treat is exciting and creative, adding to the celebration of your favorite villain—such as the evil sea witch Ursala or the hot-headed Hades—whether you prepare a meal for one or a gathering of friends and family.

While acting the part of a diabolical Villain may be bad for your health, the recipes in this book are purely good and wholesome. Recipes with a Nutritious Tip are simply healthful takes on traditional meals. You'll find recipes that call for healthful fruits, vegetables, and plant-based proteins—as well as ingredients that have reduced sodium, sugar, and unhealthy fats.

Whether you're feeling as regal as Lady Tremaine, as egocentric as Gaston, as diabolical as Scar, or as cruel as Cruella de Vil herself, these sinful snacks, hellishly hearty meals, and devilish dishes are sure to inspire your most wonderfully wicked schemes.

Cooking Tips

Many of the recipes in this book have beginners in mind. If you're just learning your way around the kitchen, you might want to start out with these easy recipes.

Appetizers: Flotsam & Jetsam Party Mix, Pint of Ale Cheese Bowl

Breakfast: Dozen Egg Breakfast, Underworld Smoothie

Salads & Sides: Horrible Wholesome Sunshine Salad, Golden Strands of Spaghetti Squash

Main Courses: Chicken Soup for Sick Dragons, Jolly Roger Brisket

Cakes & Pies: Molten Lava Cakes

Cookies & Sweets: Hypnotizing Snake Staffs, Tiger Tails

Drinks: Peddler's Disguise, Painting the Frozé Red

If you're ready to start out in the kitchen, here are a few tips that will help you find your way.

1) Remember That Everyone Starts Somewhere

Even the most accomplished gourmet chefs started out by learning tips and tricks in the kitchen from people who had been cooking a long time and who had more experience. What's true for people cooking at home is the same as people who have gone on to run restaurants, write cookbooks, cook on television, and define what the world thinks of as delicious. That truth: We all learn and get better with practice.

2) Ask for Help

If you're stuck on something or don't understand directions, the best thing you can do is ask for help. Your parents or grandparents can easily help you work through something.

3) Search Online for Cooking Tutorials

You can also easily search for cooking help on the internet. If you want a quick lesson in caramelizing onions, melting chocolate, making whipped cream, or muddling fruit, you can find lots and lots of video demonstrations by professional chefs online.

4) Work Your Way Up to Harder Recipes

As you get more comfortable in the kitchen—and with following recipes—you'll feel more confident in trying more challenging creations. The most complicated recipes in this book are Olympus Moussaka (which requires preparing vegetables in several ways and making a béchamel sauce), Snake Pie (which uses phyllo dough and can be tricky to work with the first few times), and Voodoo Top Hat Cake (which calls for a cake decorated in rolled fondant, which also requires some practice).

5) Try to Be Patient

Don't get frustrated if your dish doesn't work out the first time. It takes a *lot* of practice to make challenging recipes.

6) Let Your Creativity Shine

Following a recipe is important when it comes to cooking times and order of steps—but when it comes to making a dish truly great, that comes from you. Experiment in the kitchen. Substitute ingredients that you love for unfamiliar or disliked ingredients to suit yourself as well as anyone else who will be eating the dish. Do you like white chocolate better than dark? Grapes more than strawberries? Basil more than oregano? Great. Use flavors you already love as a guide to what you think will make a recipe perfect for you.

Appetizers

Crabulous Crab Dip

Flotsam & Jetsam Party Mix

"Palm of My Hand" Pies

Deviled Dragon Eggs

Pretty Polly Crackers & Hummus

Pint of Ale Cheese Bowl

Crabulous Crab Dip

PREP TIME: 5 MINUTES | COOK TIME: 25 MINUTES | YIELD: 10

Tamatoa just can't help but brag about his knack for hoarding all kinds of shiny treasures. He sings and boasts of these sparkling finds atop his shell, certain that his collection makes him truly crabulous.

   With a whole pound of crabmeat in it, this hot, cheesy dip is most definitely crabulous. Serve warm with crackers and fresh bread.

1 pound lump crabmeat

8 ounces cream cheese, softened

¼ cup sour cream

¼ cup mayonnaise

1 cup grated cheddar cheese, plus more for garnish

½ cup grated Parmesan cheese, plus more for garnish

2 cloves garlic, minced

½ teaspoon paprika

1 tablespoon Worcestershire sauce

1 tablespoon hot sauce

1 tablespoon Dijon mustard

Juice of half a lemon

¼ teaspoon salt

¼ teaspoon pepper

Preheat oven to 375°F.

Remove crab from its container and rinse well. Allow to drain.

In a medium mixing bowl, combine all ingredients and mix well.

Transfer to a medium baking dish, and garnish with cheese. Bake for 20 to 25 minutes until the top has browned and the mixture is bubbling. Serve with crackers or crostini.

NUTRITIOUS TIP: Serve the dip with a big platter of veggies, including carrots, celery, broccoli, and bell peppers.

Flotsam & Jetsam Party Mix

PREP TIME: 5 MINUTES | COOK TIME: 45 MINUTES | YIELD: 8 TO 10 SERVINGS

Ursula's "beloved babies" are Flotsam and Jetsam, moray eels who do her bidding, including enticing Ariel to go speak to the Sea Witch after King Triton destroys her grotto. In the dictionary, flotsam is defined as the wreckage of a shipwreck, and jetsam is anything that has been thrown off a ship and washed up on shore. They're fancy words for bits and pieces of things, like this sweet and savory party mix.

The beauty of making your own party mix is that you can make it anything you want it to be. Go with something salty, something cheesy, and something sweet to mix into your cereals—or go wild and use candy, popcorn, or Parmesan crisps.

Don't be afraid of the hot sauce. The amount called for in the recipe is mild in the final result. For more of a kick, use up to ½ cup of hot sauce, and add a pinch of cayenne and a bit more sugar to the mixture.

½ cup (1 stick) butter

2 teaspoons garlic powder

2 teaspoons smoked paprika

2 tablespoons Worcestershire sauce

¼ cup buffalo-style hot sauce

1½ tablespoons brown sugar

2 cups square corn cereal

2 cups square rice cereal

2 cups square cheese crackers

2 cups pretzels

1 cup dried cranberries

1 cup chocolate chips

Preheat the oven to 250°F. In a small saucepan over medium heat, melt the butter. Add the spices, Worcestershire sauce, hot sauce, and brown sugar. Cook for 2 minutes until combined.

In a large mixing bowl, combine the cereal, crackers, and pretzels. (Omit anything that will melt or won't hold up to baking for this step.) Pour the hot mixture over the contents of the bowl and mix well.

Spread the mixture over two lined baking sheets in a single layer. Bake until golden and fragrant, about 45 minutes. Remove from the oven and allow to cool.

Mix in the dried fruit and chocolate. Serve.

"Palm of My Hand" Pies

PREP TIME: 15 MINUTES | COOK TIME: 40 MINUTES | YIELD: 16 LARGE OR 30 SMALL HAND PIES

Dr. Facilier is up to his villainous tricks—like turning Prince Naveen into a frog—so he can have total control of his city. "I'll have New Orleans in the palm of my hand," he says. These hand pies can, in fact, be eaten from the palm of your hand, and are inspired by traditional New Orleans crawfish hand pies. If you can't find crawfish, substitute shrimp, and cut them into small pieces before cooking.

2 tablespoons unsalted butter

2 tablespoons flour

1 small yellow onion, minced

½ green pepper, minced

1 medium stalk celery, minced

½ teaspoon salt

½ teaspoon black pepper

1 teaspoon paprika

½ teaspoon cayenne pepper

3 cloves minced garlic

2 cups (1 pound) fresh or frozen peeled crawfish tails, thawed and drained

1 tablespoon hot sauce

1 teaspoon Worcestershire sauce

½ cup heavy cream

2 tablespoons breadcrumbs

4 sheets purchased pie dough

2 eggs, lightly beaten

In a large skillet over medium heat, make a roux by melting the butter with the flour, stirring often, until the roux deepens to a golden brown, about 5 minutes.

Add the onion, green pepper, celery, and seasonings, and sauté for about 4 minutes, until the vegetables start to soften. Add the garlic and crawfish. Cook for 2 minutes, then add hot sauce and Worcestershire sauce, and cook an additional 2 minutes.

Whisk in the cream, then add the breadcrumbs. Remove the skillet from the heat and let cool.

Preheat the oven to 375°F. Line a baking sheet with foil or parchment paper.

Roll out the pie dough. If you're making small hand pies, cut thirty 3-inch circles. If you're making large hand pies, cut sixteen 5-inch circles. Brush the outer edges of the dough with eggs, then place 2 to 4 tablespoons of filling in the center of each, depending on size.

Fold the dough over to make half-circles, then press edges together firmly with your fingers or a fork to seal. Brush the top of each with eggs. Bake until golden brown, about 25 minutes. Remove from the oven and serve warm.

Deviled Dragon Eggs

PREP TIME: 30 MINUTES | COOK TIME: 60 MINUTES | YIELD: 24 PIECES

Maleficent doesn't receive an invite to the christening of infant Princess Aurora, so what is an evil fairy to do? Curse the princess, of course, and transform into an enormous fire-breathing dragon. As such, she rains down terror upon King Stefan's kingdom and is intent on exacting her revenge. These Deviled "Dragon" Eggs may look as terrifying as Maleficent, but they're delicious and impressive.

8 cups shredded red cabbage

12 large eggs

2 tablespoons olive oil

1 tablespoon mayonnaise

1 teaspoon Dijon mustard

1 teaspoon chopped fresh dill, plus more for garnish

Salt and pepper, to taste

Place 4 cups of the shredded cabbage in a medium saucepan. Cover the cabbage so it's totally submerged in water with at least 1 inch of water above it. Boil over medium-high heat until tender and the water is deep purple, 20 to 30 minutes. Using a slotted spoon, remove the cooked shredded cabbage and discard, leaving the water in the pan.

While the cabbage is cooking, prepare the eggs. Place the eggs in a separate medium saucepan and cover with water by at least 1 inch. Over medium-high heat, bring the water to a full boil. As soon as the water is boiling, remove the pan from the heat and cover. Let the eggs sit in the hot water for 15 minutes, then remove to an ice bath to chill for 1 minute.

Lightly crack the egg shells by rolling them on a kitchen towel on the counter. You want there to be fine cracks, but for the shell to still adhere. The finer the cracks, the better the result will be, so be careful.

Place the eggs in a storage container with a lid. Pour the cabbage water over the eggs, cover, and chill for at least 12 hours or overnight.

Remove the eggs from the water, then peel the shells. The result should be beautiful purple marbling of the egg whites. Cut each egg in half lengthwise. Scoop out the yolk into a medium mixing bowl, and place the whites on a platter.

In the bowl with the yolks, add the olive oil, mayonnaise, mustard, dill, salt, and pepper. Stir to combine, then divide evenly between the cups of the egg whites.

Top eggs with a sprinkle of dill and serve eggs over nests made with the remaining raw cabbage. Chill before serving.

Pretty Polly Crackers & Hummus

PREP TIME: 20 MINUTES | COOK TIME: 45 MINUTES | YIELD: 6 SERVINGS

"Have a cracker, pretty Polly!" the Sultan gleefully exclaims as he stuffs a cracker into Iago's mouth. Iago, however, does *not* enjoy the treat. "I can't take it anymore!" Jafar's evil parrot sidekick shouts as they walk into Jafar's lair. "If I gotta choke on one more of those moldy, disgusting crackers... BAM! WHAP!"

FOR THE HUMMUS

One 14.5-ounce can chickpeas, drained

¼ cup tahini paste

1 clove garlic

Juice of 1 lemon

1 large roasted red pepper, seeded and sliced

½ teaspoon salt, plus more to taste

3 tablespoons olive oil

FOR THE CRACKERS

1 large head cauliflower, cut into florets

2 tablespoons ground flaxseeds

2 cups brown rice flour

½ teaspoon salt

1 teaspoon garlic powder

Sesame seeds, optional

Prepare the hummus. Combine the chickpeas, tahini, garlic, lemon juice, red pepper, and salt in the bowl of a food processor. (For a smoother hummus, remove the skins from the chickpeas first.) Mix for 2 minutes. While the processor is running, slowly pour the olive oil into the pour spout. Mix for 2 minutes more. For creamier texture, add 2 tablespoons of cold water and mix for 1 minute more. Remove to a bowl, then cover and refrigerate at least 1 hour.

Prepare the crackers. Preheat the oven to 400°F. In a large saucepan fitted with a steamer basket, add water to just below the bottom of the steamer, then add cauliflower to the basket. Cover and bring to a boil. Steam until cauliflower is soft, about 10 minutes. Remove from heat and allow to cool slightly. Reserve ¼ cup of cooking liquid.

While the cauliflower is cooling, add the flaxseeds, rice flour, salt, and garlic powder to the clean bowl of a food processor. Add cauliflower and mix on high, slowly pouring in the cooking liquid until a smooth batter forms. Rest for 10 minutes for flaxseeds to thicken the batter.

Line two baking sheets with parchment paper. Divide batter evenly between sheets, and spread using a spatula to the very edges of the paper to ensure even cooking. Score the batter into 2-by-2-inch squares. Sprinkle with sesame seeds, if using. Bake about 15 minutes, then flip the crackers over, swap positions of the sheet pans in the oven, and bake another 15 to 20 minutes until golden and crispy. Serve with hummus.

NUTRITIOUS TIP: These crackers are anything but "moldy and disgusting." They're flavorful and healthy, made mostly of cauliflower with a bit of rice flour and ground flaxseeds. Both the crackers and roasted red pepper hummus are totally vegan and gluten-free, and full of plant-based protein and veggies.

Pint of Ale Cheese Bowl

PREP TIME: 5 MINUTES | COOK TIME: 10 MINUTES | YIELD: 6 SERVINGS

Gaston loves three things: himself, hunting (for his dinner and for a wife), and raising a pint of ale at the pub with LeFou. This dip is as cheesy as Gaston himself. If you can't find a bread boule at the grocery store, you should be able to find one at a bakery—but if not, just serve in a regular bowl with bread and veggies to dip.

3 tablespoons butter

¼ cup all-purpose flour

1 cup milk

1 cup lager beer or ale

1 teaspoon dry mustard

1 teaspoon garlic powder

½ teaspoon salt

½ teaspoon cayenne pepper, or more to taste

3 cups bold shredded cheese, such as sharp cheddar or Swiss

Large round loaf of bread (bread boule)

Carrot sticks, celery sticks, and other cut-up vegetables for dipping

In a medium saucepan over medium heat, melt the butter and flour together to make a roux. Cook for 3 minutes, whisking constantly. Slowly whisk in the milk to avoid clumping. Add the beer and spices, and allow to cook for 3 minutes. Whisk in the cheese, and cook for 5 minutes, whisking often. Remove from the heat once cheese is melted and smoothly combined.

Using a serrated knife, hollow out the center of the bread, making sure not to pierce the bottom. Make a large enough "bowl" to hold all the cheese. (Or, if your loaf is smaller, to hold half of it and reserve half the cheese to refill later.) Cut the bread you've removed into bite-size pieces for dipping.

Place the bread boule in the center of the platter, then arrange bread pieces and veggies around it. Pour the hot cheese into the boule and serve.

Breakfast

Lady Tremaine Toast

Monkey's Uncle Monkey Bread

Dalmatian Pancakes with Strawberry Compote

Poor Unfortunate Rolls

Underworld Smoothie

Dozen Egg Breakfast

Lady Tremaine Toast

PREP TIME: 20 MINUTES | COOK TIME: 60 MINUTES | YIELD: 8 TO 10 SERVINGS

Cinderella's wicked stepmother, Lady Tremaine, indulges in a luxurious breakfast while her step-daughter dusts and mops. This delicious breakfast of lemon curd and lemon-lavender cake is inspired by the French countryside. The lemon curd, a nice balance of sweet and tart, is easily adjusted for more sweetness or more citrus.

FOR THE LEMON-LAVENDER POUND CAKE

1 cup granulated sugar

2 teaspoons dried culinary lavender

Zest of 2 lemons

½ cup (1 stick) unsalted butter, softened

2 large eggs

1½ cups all-purpose flour

¾ teaspoon salt

¾ teaspoon baking powder

¼ teaspoon baking soda

½ cup milk

Juice of 2 lemons

1 teaspoon vanilla extract

Nonstick cooking spray

FOR THE LEMON CURD

Juice of 4 lemons

Zest of 1 lemon

½ cup sugar

1 tablespoon cornstarch

3 eggs

6 tablespoons (¾ stick) butter, cut into chunks

Prepare the pound cake. Preheat the oven to 350°F. In the bowl of a food processor, combine the sugar, lavender, and lemon zest. Pulse or process until the lavender is finely chopped.

Transfer to the bowl of a stand mixer and add the butter. Whip until light and fluffy, about 5 minutes. Add the eggs and mix another 3 minutes.

In a medium mixing bowl, combine the flour, salt, baking powder, and baking soda. In another, combine the milk, lemon juice, and vanilla.

While mixer is running, add half the dry mixture to the bowl and mix 1 minute. Add the liquid and mix another minute. Add the remaining dry mixture and mix 1 more minute.

Spray a standard loaf pan with cooking spray. Pour batter into pan. Bake until a knife inserted into center comes out clean, about 50 minutes. Do not overbake or the cake will be dry. Remove to a wire rack to cool.

While the cake is baking, prepare the lemon curd. Fill a large saucepan with a few inches of water, then place a double boiler or a medium mixing bowl on top. (If using a bowl, make sure the edges of the pan fit tightly to the sides of the bowl and the bottom of the bowl doesn't touch the water.)

Over medium-high heat, add the lemon juice, lemon zest, sugar, cornstarch, and eggs to the bowl. Whisk nearly constantly until the mixture thickens and turns bright yellow, about 10 minutes. You should see this happen *just* as the mixture starts to bubble around the edges. Do not let the eggs cook. Remove from heat and whisk in the butter until melted. Chill until ready to serve.

Turn the pound cake out onto a cutting board once cooled and slice. Serve with a generous spoonful of lemon curd.

Monkey's Uncle Monkey Bread

PREP TIME: 2½ HOURS | COOK TIME: 40 MINUTES | YIELD: 6 SERVINGS

Scar is less than enthusiastic at the prospect that his nephew Simba will one day become the king of Pride Rock. When Simba asks Scar what his uncle will be once the young cub is finally king, Scar replies, "A monkey's uncle." Filled with jealousy, the vengeful lion begins to plot his brother's downfall in order to become the ruler of Pride Rock.

FOR THE DOUGH

1½ cups milk

1 package fast-rising yeast

¼ cup granulated sugar

3 large eggs

1 teaspoon vanilla extract

1½ teaspoons salt

5 cups flour

Nonstick cooking spray

FOR THE MONKEY BREAD

1 cup granulated sugar

2 tablespoons ground cinnamon

2 bananas, sliced

1 cup (2 sticks) melted butter

Nonstick cooking spray

Prepare the dough. In a small saucepan over medium heat, bring the milk to a simmer. Do not boil. Remove from heat and whisk in the yeast and sugar. Cover the saucepan and let stand for about 10 minutes to activate the yeast.

Transfer the mixture to the bowl of a stand mixer fitted with a dough hook, then mix in the eggs, vanilla, and salt by hand. Mix on low setting and gradually add the flour, working slowly so all ingredients combine well. Turn the speed to medium and mix the dough until it starts to pull away from the sides of the bowl. Mix 2 minutes more to knead the dough.

Place the dough in a bowl sprayed with cooking spray; cover, and let rise for 2 hours until doubled in size. Punch dough down, then turn it out onto a work surface and slice into 1-inch chunks. (If using premade dough, start here.)

Prepare the Monkey Bread. Preheat the oven to 350°F. In a medium bowl, combine the sugar and cinnamon. Spray a Bundt pan liberally with cooking spray. Roll each piece of the dough in the cinnamon-sugar, then add to the pan, layering along with the banana slices, and ending with a layer of dough pieces.

Sprinkle remaining cinnamon-sugar over dough, then drizzle with melted butter. Bake for 40 minutes, then remove from the oven. Place a plate over the top of the monkey bread, then flip onto the plate. Let stand 3 minutes, then remove the Bundt pan. Let stand about 10 minutes before serving.

NUTRITIOUS TIP: This healthier version of Monkey Bread has bananas in the mix and uses fresh, unprocessed dough. (If you use store-bought dough, buy 4 standard-size canisters of biscuit dough.) Enjoy it with your monkeys—er, your family.

Dalmatian Pancakes with Strawberry Compote

PREP TIME: 20 MINUTES | COOK TIME: 25 MINUTES | YIELDS: 8 TO 10 PANCAKES

Cruella De Vil simply cannot live without furs, or so she says. Ever in the pursuit of those puppies as well as high fashion, Cruella races through the countryside—a vision of black, white, and red.

These delicious pancakes are a riff on dalmatian cookies, with a vivid red strawberry compote that brings to mind the black, white, and red of Cruella's classic look, without any of the evil.

FOR THE STRAWBERRY COMPOTE

1 pound strawberries

½ cup sugar

Juice of half a lemon

½ teaspoon vanilla bean paste

FOR THE PANCAKES

1 cup all-purpose flour

2 teaspoons baking powder

½ teaspoon salt

2 tablespoons sugar

1 cup milk

1 egg, beaten

2 tablespoons butter, melted

1 teaspoon vanilla extract

¼ cup white chocolate chips

¼ cup milk chocolate chips

Nonstick cooking spray

Prepare the strawberry compote. Wash and chop the strawberries, discarding stems and hulls of the fruit. Combine fruit with remaining ingredients in a medium saucepan. Bring to a boil over medium heat, then reduce to a simmer and cook about 15 minutes, until fruit has softened and sauce has thickened. Remove from heat and set aside to cool.

Prepare the pancakes. In a mixing bowl, combine the dry ingredients. Add the wet ingredients, and stir to combine. Let stand 10 minutes.

Heat a large skillet over medium. Off the burner, spray it with nonstick cooking spray. Drop batter by a ¼-cup measuring cup into pan, being careful not to crowd pancakes.

Cook until golden brown and bubbles rise to the surface, about 3 minutes. Flip, and cook another 2 to 3 minutes, until golden brown. Remove from heat and transfer to a plate tented with aluminum foil to keep pancakes warm. Repeat with remaining batter. Serve topped with strawberry compote and, if desired, additional white and milk chocolate chips.

Poor Unfortunate Rolls

PREP TIME: 15 MINUTES | COOK TIME: 30 MINUTES | YIELDS: 12 ROLLS

Ursula boasts that she helps "poor unfortunate souls," though her idea of being helpful is anything but! Once ensnared by the sea witch, these souls have little hope of escaping her clutches. Like Ursula's promises of beauty, happiness, and love, these cinnamon rolls are oh, so tempting. If you can't find purple food coloring, combine red and blue until you achieve the desired hue.

FOR THE CINNAMON ROLLS

3 to 3½ cups all-purpose flour, plus more for dusting

½ cup granulated sugar

1 teaspoon salt

1 packet instant yeast

½ cup butter, divided, at room temperature

⅔ cup whole milk

¼ cup water

1 large egg

1 tablespoon ground cinnamon

½ teaspoon nutmeg

½ cup light brown sugar

Nonstick cooking spray

FOR THE ICING

1 cup confectioners' sugar

1 teaspoon vanilla extract

2 tablespoons milk

Purple food coloring

Prepare the dough. In a large mixing bowl, whisk together the flour, granulated sugar, salt, and yeast. Set aside.

In a small saucepan over medium heat, combine ¼ cup butter, the milk, and the water. Heat until butter is melted and liquid is warm.

Pour the liquid into the dry ingredients, then add the egg. Stir until a soft dough forms.

On a lightly floured surface, knead the dough for 5 minutes, then cover and let rest for 10 minutes.

Prepare the filling. In a microwave-safe bowl, heat the remaining ¼ cup butter until melted; add the cinnamon, nutmeg, and brown sugar, and stir until combined.

Using a rolling pin, roll the dough into a 16-by-10-inch rectangle. Spread the filling on the dough, then roll one long edge of dough toward opposite side, enclosing filling and pinching dough to seal seam.

Cut dough into 12 even pieces, and place them in a 9-by-13-inch baking dish sprayed with nonstick cooking spray. Wrap with plastic wrap and let rolls rise until doubled in size, 60 to 90 minutes.

Preheat oven to 375°F. Bake for 28 to 30 minutes or until lightly browned. Remove from oven.

Prepare the icing. Whisk together the confectioners' sugar, vanilla, and milk. Add enough purple food coloring to reach desired hue. Spread icing on warm rolls.

Underworld Smoothies

PREP TIME: 10 MINUTES | YIELD: 2 SERVINGS

"If there's one god you don't want to get steamed up, it's Hades, 'cause he had an evil plan," the Muses sing. "He ran the underworld, but thought the dead were dull and uncouth. He was as mean as he was ruthless, and that's the gospel truth." But Hades *does* get steamed up all the time, especially when his evil plans to defeat Hercules are thwarted.

This healthy breakfast smoothie plays on Hades' two moods: When he's calm, he has blue flames for hair; when he's angry, those flames turn red. Mix each recipe separately, then pour both in the same glass to get a true representation of Hades' feelings.

FOR THE CALM BLUE SMOOTHIE

1 cup frozen blueberries

½ cup frozen blackberries

¼ cup plain Greek yogurt

½ cup grape, blueberry, or blackberry juice

1 cup ice

FOR THE ANGRY RED SMOOTHIE

1 cup frozen strawberries

½ cup frozen raspberries

¼ cup plain Greek yogurt

½ cup strawberry, cranberry, or beet juice

1 cup ice

Combine all the ingredients for the blue smoothie in a blender, and blend until combined. Pour into a measuring cup with a pouring lip and set aside.

Combine all the ingredients for the red smoothie in a blender, and blend until combined.

Holding a vessel in each hand, pour half the two smoothies into a drinking glass at the same time, then repeat with a second glass. Enjoy cold.

NUTRITIOUS TIP: Fruits like blueberries contain high levels of antioxidants. Antioxidants can help protect your body against free radicals, which can contribute to diseases.

Dozen Egg Breakfast

PREP TIME: 10 MINUTES | COOK TIME: 20 MINUTES | YIELD: 12 PIECES

Gaston says he eats five dozen eggs every day, but that might be a little too much for anyone who isn't "roughly the size of a barge." This breakfast calls for a dozen eggs, and that's enough for a few days of morning meals. To make them last more than a day or two, freeze each one individually, then microwave from frozen about 1 minute, wrapped in a damp paper towel, for a quick breakfast on the go.

Nonstick cooking spray

½ small onion, diced

¼ cup chopped broccoli

1 dozen large eggs

½ teaspoon salt

½ teaspoon black pepper

½ teaspoon garlic powder

4 slices bacon, cooked and crumbled

½ cup shredded cheese

Preheat the oven to 350°F. Spray a 12-cup muffin tin with nonstick cooking spray.

Spray a medium skillet with cooking spray. Over medium heat, sauté the onion until beginning to soften, about 3 minutes, then add the broccoli and cook another 2 minutes until soft and bright green. Set aside.

In a large mixing bowl, beat the eggs until combined. Add the spices, bacon, cheese, and vegetables; then stir to mix.

Evenly distribute the filling among the 12 cups of the muffin tin. Bake until cooked and light brown, about 20 minutes. Serve, or freeze individually for quick breakfasts.

Salads & Sides

Croquet Croquettes

Golden Strands of Spaghetti Squash

The Golden Rule Treasure Pasta Salad

Horrible Wholesome Sunshine Salad

Lion's Share Farro Salad

Sea Witch Shrimp Kebabs

Spinning Wheel Potatoes

Magic Flower Salad

Croquet Croquettes

PREP TIME: 30 MINUTES | COOK TIME: 20 MINUTES | YIELD: 46 CROQUETTES

"Do you play croquet?" the Queen of Hearts asks Alice.

"Why yes, your majesty," she replies.

"Then let the games begin!"

These croquettes are a delicious side or snack, before or after croquet—no beheadings necessary. Add some ham or broccoli (or both!) for variety.

5 medium russet potatoes, peeled and coarsely chopped

¼ cup (½ stick) butter

1 cup shredded sharp cheddar cheese

2 egg yolks

1½ tablespoons dried parsley

½ teaspoon salt

½ teaspoon pepper

1 cup all-purpose flour

2 whole eggs

1 cup seasoned breadcrumbs

1 to 2 cups vegetable oil, for frying

In a large saucepan over high heat, cook the potatoes in boiling water until soft. Drain and transfer to a large mixing bowl. Add the butter and mash using a potato masher. Add the cheese and stir until combined. Let cool for 5 minutes. Add the egg yolks, parsley, salt, and pepper, and stir until combined. Form into approximately 46 (2-inch) balls.

Set out three small bowls. In one, place the flour. In another bowl, beat the whole eggs. In a third bowl, place the breadcrumbs. Roll each croquette in flour, then eggs, then breadcrumbs. Set aside.

In a large skillet with high sides, heat 1 cup of cooking oil over medium-high heat. Working in batches, fry the croquettes until golden brown, about 2 to 3 minutes per side. Drain on paper towels and serve hot.

NUTRITIOUS TIP: Instead of frying, the croquettes can be baked for 20 minutes at 375°F. If baking, drizzle the croquettes with oil before putting them in the oven.

Golden Strands of Spaghetti Squash

PREP TIME: 5 MINUTES | COOK TIME: 60 MINUTES | YIELD: 4 SERVINGS

The ever-envious Mother Gothel covets the magic in Rapunzel's extraordinary hair so much that she steals the baby away and locks her in a tower so no one else can access the magic in Rapunzel's strands. Spaghetti squash, one of the easiest to prepare and a very versatile vegetable, resembles Rapunzel's strands after it's cooked.

1 medium spaghetti squash
(2 to 3 pounds)
¼ cup (½ stick) butter
3 tablespoons fresh thyme
Salt and pepper to taste

Preheat the oven to 400°F. Using a fork, pierce the skin all over. Bake, whole, directly on the oven rack, about 45 minutes or, up to 1 hour, depending on the size of squash. To test for doneness, pierce with a fork through the squash skin.

Remove from the oven. When the squash is cool enough to handle, cut it in half, then gently scrape out the seeds and pith with a spoon.

Starting from center, use a fork to draw against the squash pulp, creating strands. Try to avoid large clumps. Remove to a bowl.

If the squash is still warm, toss it with the butter, thyme, salt, and pepper until the butter has melted. If the squash is cool, transfer it to a medium skillet over low heat and toss with butter, thyme, salt, and pepper before serving.

NUTRITIOUS TIP: This simple preparation uses fresh herbs and a little bit of butter—but you could swap out the thyme for any herbs you like, or add some Parmesan or goat cheese for protein.

The Golden Rule Treasure Pasta Salad

PREP TIME: 5 MINUTES | COOK TIME: 10 MINUTES | YIELD: 6 SERVINGS

"You've heard of the golden rule, haven't you?" Jafar asks Aladdin when they're in the Sultan's dungeon. "Whoever has the gold makes the rules." They escape, and the evil sorcerer sends Aladdin into the Cave of Wonders, full of treasures beyond imagining, in search of the most prized treasure of them all: the Genie's lamp.

The "treasure" in this light pasta salad comes from pearl pasta, and the "gold" comes from golden tomatoes. In place of either one, any small pasta and any small tomato will do. You can easily prep this salad ahead of serving—just leave off the fresh herbs until ready to serve.

2 cups pearl pasta

Juice of 1 lemon

¼ cup olive oil

2 tablespoons red wine
    vinegar

½ teaspoon salt

½ teaspoon black pepper

1 cup small yellow tomatoes

½ cup crumbled feta cheese

¼ cup chopped mint

2 tablespoons chopped
    fresh parsley

Cook the pasta according to package directions. Drain if necessary. Set aside in a medium serving bowl.

In a small bowl, whisk together the lemon juice, olive oil, vinegar, salt, and pepper until combined. Drizzle over the pasta and mix well.

Stir in tomatoes, cheese, and herbs if serving immediately. If making ahead, stir in tomatoes and cheese, cover, chill, then stir in herbs right before serving.

Horrible Wholesome Sunshine Salad

PREP TIME: 10 MINUTES | YIELD: 4 SERVINGS

"Someone's sick!" Madam Mim exclaims when she hears Wort coughing after he's fallen down the chimney of her cottage. "How lovely!" She isn't quite so happy, though, when she loses the Wizard's Duel to Merlin and ends up sick in bed herself. "It's not too serious, Madam, you should be recovered in a couple of weeks and be as good... I mean, as bad as ever," Merlin says. "I would suggest plenty of rest and lots and lots of sunshine."

"I hate sunshine!" Madam Mim says. "I hate horrible wholesome sunshine! I hate it!"

This salad isn't exactly made of sunshine, but it *is* made of bright, fresh citrus. Choose your favorites for this recipe: a mix of sweet navel oranges, blood oranges, ruby red grapefruit, and pomelos mix well together, or you can customize to taste. A touch of Meyer lemon would add zesty tang, depending on how much you love horrible wholesome sunshine!

8 naval oranges, blood oranges, and/or grapefruit

2 tablespoons honey

2 tablespoons apple cider vinegar

¼ cup olive oil

Salt and pepper, to taste

2 tablespoons chopped fresh mint,

1 tablespoon chopped fresh basil

3 tablespoons crumbled feta or goat cheese

Prepare the citrus. Peel each fruit with a knife, making sure to remove all the pith, then cut slices about ¼ inch thick. Arrange on a serving tray.

Prepare the dressing. In a small bowl, combine the honey, vinegar, olive oil, salt, and pepper. Whisk until emulsified.

Drizzle the dressing over the fruit, then top with the herbs and cheese. Serve immediately.

Lion's Share Farro Salad

PREP TIME: 15 MINUTES | COOK TIME: 30 MINUTES | YIELD: 4 SERVINGS

Instead of attending the presentation of his nephew Simba at Pride Rock, jealous Scar sulks in his cave. Mufasa confronts his wayward brother, and the two lions nearly get into a fight. "Temper, temper. I wouldn't dream of challenging you," Scar says. "As far as brains go, I got the lion's share, but when it comes to brute strength, I'm afraid I'm at the shallow end of the gene pool."

3 pounds assorted root vegetables, such as sweet potatoes, parsnips, onions, beets, and/or carrots

½ cup olive oil, divided

1 teaspoon salt, plus more to taste

½ teaspoon pepper, plus more to taste

2 cups cooked farro, prepared according to package directions

6 tablespoons red wine vinegar

2 cups baby arugula

Preheat the oven to 425°F.

Wash and, if needed, peel the vegetables. Chop into bite-size pieces, keeping pieces similar size for even cooking. Toss with ¼ cup olive oil and the salt and pepper. Spread in an even layer on a large baking sheet, and roast until crisp-tender, about 30 minutes, tossing once halfway through. Remove from oven and allow to cool slightly.

In a medium bowl, toss the farro, remaining olive oil, vinegar, and more salt and pepper to taste. Mix in the arugula just before serving, then top with roasted vegetables. Serve warm or cold.

NUTRITIOUS TIP: This Lion's Share Farro Salad is a smart choice in more ways than one: It's easy to make, it has loads of flavor, plus it's a protein-rich vegetarian side that could easily be a main course for Meatless Monday. Use a variety of root vegetables, and don't be afraid to leave peels on (edible peels, that is) or include a few veggies that you don't normally like. You might be pleasantly surprised at how well everything comes together in this dish.

Sea Witch Shrimp Kebabs

PREP TIME: 15 MINUTES | COOK TIME: 5 MINUTES | YIELD: 6 SERVINGS

"In my day, we had fantastical feasts when I lived in the palace," Ursula laments as she snacks on shrimp. "And now look at me, wasted away to practically nothing. Banished and exiled and practically starving."

These spicy shrimp kebabs fit right in to Ursula's lair. Delicious on a salad or served alongside a grilled steak for a special occasion dinner—they're so easy to make that you definitely won't need to wait for a special occasion.

2 pounds large shrimp, peeled and deveined

3 large cloves garlic, minced

1½ teaspoon coarse salt

½ teaspoons cayenne pepper

¼ teaspoon crushed red pepper

1 teaspoon paprika

3 tablespoons olive oil

Juice of half a lemon

Soak six large bamboo skewers in water for at least 30 minutes to prevent skewers from burning.

In a large glass bowl, combine all ingredients. Cover and marinate in refrigerator at least 1 hour.

Divide the shrimp evenly among each skewer, about 4 or 5 pieces each.

Line the grill surface with aluminum foil, then heat the grill to medium-high. Grill the kebabs until cooked through, about 2 minutes per side. (To prepare them in the oven instead, set the oven to broil and cook for 2 minutes on each side.) Serve as a complement to a salad or vegetables, or as an appetizer.

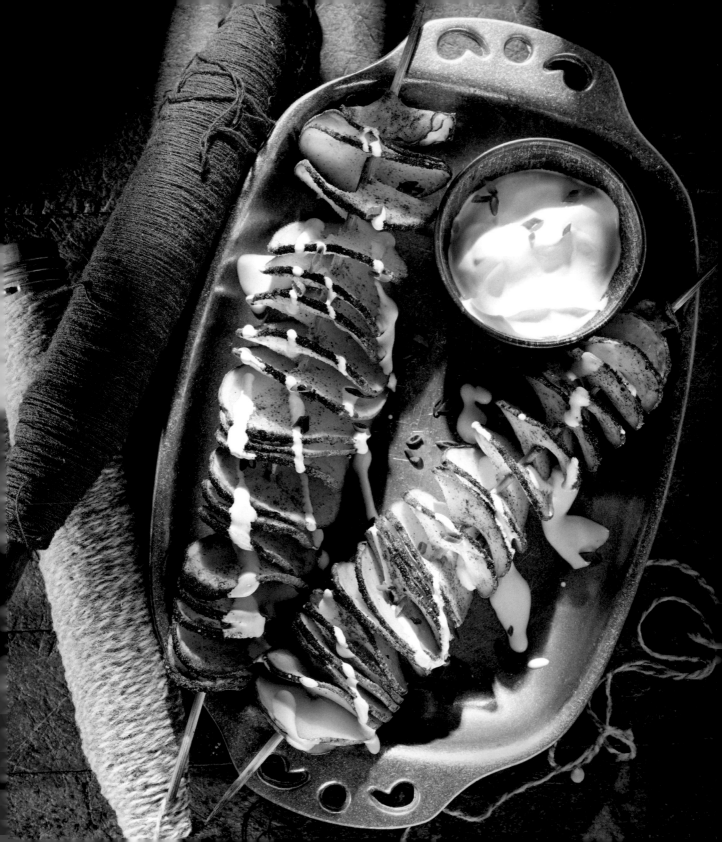

Spinning Wheel Potatoes

PREP TIME: 10 MINUTES | COOK TIME: 1 HOUR | YIELD: 4 POTATOES

"But before the sun sets on her 16th birthday, she shall prick her finger on the spindle of a spinning wheel... and die." Maleficent's curse upon the princess sets young Aurora's fate in motion. Though her parents try to protect her, the princess eventually falls into Maleficent's trap.

The stakes aren't *quite* as high here, but be careful when you make these Spinning Wheel Potatoes: You could actually prick your finger while making them. Metal skewers, the only ones that will easily pierce through a potato, can be sharp—and then there's the tricky maneuver of spiraling them with a paring knife if you don't have a spiralizer. It gets easier with practice, but in the beginning, definitely make sure to use a kitchen towel or gloves for protection. The result—a healthier baked take on a tornado potato—is worth the hard work.

4 medium russet potatoes
(about 5 ounces each),
ends trimmed

¼ cup olive oil

1 teaspoon garlic powder

½ teaspoon onion powder

½ teaspoon smoked paprika

1 teaspoon salt

½ teaspoon cayenne
pepper

½ teaspoon black pepper

Sour cream, for serving

Chives, for serving

Preheat the oven to 425°F. Soak six large bamboo skewers in water for at least 30 minutes to prevent skewers from burning.

Use the straight blade (or ribbon blade, depending on the spiralizer) to cut the potato into a thinly sliced accordion.

Carefully pierce all the way through the spiralized potatoes with bamboo skewers. Gently space rings of spiralized potato along skewers for even roasting. Drizzle with the olive oil, rotating the skewers to coat.

In a small bowl, combine the spices. Sprinkle the mixture evenly on the potatoes.

Line a medium baking dish with foil. Place the skewers on top of the dish so the ends rest on the edges and the potatoes are suspended over the bottom.

Bake until crispy, about 1 hour. Serve topped with sour cream and chives.

Magic Flower Salad

PREP TIME: 15 MINUTES | COOK TIME: 4 MINUTES | YIELD: 4 SERVINGS

"Once upon a time," the story goes, "a single drop of sunlight fell from the heavens. And from this drop of sunlight grew a magic golden flower." That flower, her own personal fountain of youth, was kept hidden away by Mother Gothel for hundreds of years. All she needed to do was sing a special song to the flower to unleash its magic: "Flower, gleam and glow, let your power shine, make the clock reverse, bring back what once was mine."

The flowers in this salad aren't magical, but they *are* unique. Squash blossoms, the edible flowers that bloom on squash and zucchini plants, appear only during summer. That you can have them only during one season makes them special. They're usually available at farmers markets, but if you can't find them, other edible flowers like nasturtiums are easy to order online.

1 small zucchini

¼ cup olive oil

¼ cup white wine vinegar

Juice of 1 lemon

1 teaspoon salt

½ teaspoon pepper

1 ear of corn, husked

4 cups salad greens such as baby arugula or butter lettuce

½ cup ciligene (pearl-size fresh mozzarella) or 1 ball fresh mozzarella, sliced

4 squash blossoms, stems and pistils removed

Use a mandoline to slice the zucchini into thin rounds. (If doing this by hand, cut slices as thin as possible.)

In a medium bowl, combine the oil, vinegar, lemon, salt, and pepper. Add the zucchini, and allow to marinate while you prepare the rest of the salad.

In a medium pot over high heat, cook the corn in boiling water until done, about 4 minutes. Remove to cool, then slice the kernels off the cob. Add the corn to the zucchini.

Divide the salad greens among 4 bowls, and top with the vegetable mixture. Add mozzarella to each, then top with 1 squash blossom. (It looks beautiful to keep the flowers whole, but it's easier to eat if you slice the flowers into thin strips.)

Main Courses

Jolly Roger Brisket

Huntsman's Pie

Pure Paragon Beef Stew

Friends on the Other Side Gumbo

Fish Dinner

Hazelnut Soup

Olympus Moussaka

Chicken Soup for Sick Dragons

Codfish and Chips

Jolly Roger Brisket

PREP TIME: 20 MINUTES | COOK TIME: 4 HOURS | YIELD: 6 SERVINGS

When Peter Pan and Captain Hook sword fight at Skull Rock, they each have a cheering section. Wendy watches (and sometimes covers her eyes) Peter's flying maneuvers, and Mr. Smee—Hook's loyal first mate—cheers on the captain. After Peter tricks Smee into shooting the Captain, Hook climbs onto a precipice to go after him again. "Give it to him, Captain!" Smee shouts. "Cleave him to the brisket."

2 tablespoons neutral cooking oil, divided

5 medium yellow onions, cut in half and into thin slices

3 to 4 pounds beef brisket

Salt and pepper

8 cloves garlic, minced

8 ounces white or baby bella mushrooms, cleaned and sliced

3 cups low-sodium beef broth

1 cup red wine

2 tablespoons Worcestershire sauce

Prepared mashed potatoes

Preheat the oven to 325°F.

In a large Dutch oven over medium heat, add 1 tablespoon cooking oil and the onions. Sauté until golden brown and caramelized, about 12 minutes. Remove to a bowl and set aside.

Pat the brisket dry with paper towels, then season generously with salt and pepper. In the same Dutch oven over high heat, add the remaining 1 tablespoon cooking oil, and sear the brisket on each side until deeply browned, about 3 minutes per side. It will smoke—turn on your oven hood or open the windows. Remove from the heat.

Add the onions, garlic, and mushrooms to the Dutch oven, then add the liquids. Cover and roast until fork-tender, about 4 hours.

Remove from the oven and let rest, covered, for 15 minutes. Remove brisket to a cutting board and discard any fat. Slice and serve with mashed potatoes, and vegetables; spoon juices over the meat.

Huntsman's Pie

PREP TIME: 45 MINUTES | COOK TIME: 1 HOUR 45 MINUTES | YIELD: 8 SERVINGS

"Magic mirror on the wall," the Queen asks her enchanted mirror every day, "who's the fairest one of all?" When the mirror answers that Snow White is "more fair than thee," the queen takes action. "Take her far into the forest," the Queen says to her Huntsman, "find some secluded place where she can pick wildflowers ... and there, my faithful Huntsman, you will kill her."

This traditional and flavorful British dish has a golden flaky crust that's simple to make. Served for special occasions, such as Sunday dinner with family and guests, it makes a beautiful presentation, with the possibility of welcomed leftovers.

FOR THE CRUST

3 cups all-purpose flour

1 teaspoon salt

¾ cup (1½ sticks) chilled butter, cut into cubes

⅔ cup ice water

1 egg, beaten (to brush on crust before baking)

FOR THE FILLINGS

8 ounces thick-cut bacon, cut into ¼-by-1-inch strips

1 large celery stalk, minced

1 medium yellow onion, minced

2 tablespoons minced fresh Italian parsley,

2 teaspoons dried sage

5 slices white bread, cut into cubes

½ cup chicken or vegetable stock

1 teaspoon salt

1 teaspoon pepper

1 pound ground chicken

1 pound ground pork

½ teaspoon dried nutmeg

Nonstick cooking spray, red food coloring

Prepare the crust. In the bowl of a food processor, combine the flour, salt, and butter, and process until the mixture resembles sand. While food processor is running, slowly pour in the water until a dough forms. Turn dough out onto a work surface, then knead briefly, five or six turns. Divide dough into two portions: one-third and two-thirds. Cover and refrigerate dough at least 30 minutes.

While dough is chilling, prepare the filling. In a large skillet over medium heat, cook the bacon until it begins to crisp. Remove to a lined plate, and drain most of the fat from the pan.

In the same skillet, cook the celery and onion until softened, about 10 minutes. Remove to a large mixing bowl. Add the parsley, sage, bread, stock, salt, and pepper. Stir to combine, then add the ground chicken. Stir to combine (this may be easier with your hands).

In another large mixing bowl, combine the bacon, pork, and nutmeg.

continued on page 60

continued from page 59

Position oven racks in lower third and upper third of oven. Preheat oven to 325°F. Spray the inside of a 10-inch springform pan with cooking spray. Using a rolling pin on a work surface, roll the larger portion of dough into a 16-inch circle. Place in the pan, pressing dough into corners and up the sides of the pan. Spread the pork filling on the dough, then spread the chicken filling on top.

Roll remaining dough into a 10-inch circle (reserving a small piece of dough for heart decoration), and place on fillings. Press crust edges firmly together; pinch edges to seal. Cut a few slits in the top of the crust to allow steam to escape, then brush with the beaten egg. With reserved piece of dough, cut out a heart shape and place on crust. Add red food coloring to remaining egg wash and brush on the heart.

Place springform pan on a rimmed baking sheet. Bake pie on the lower rack of the oven for 1 hour, then transfer to the top rack to bake until golden brown, about 45 minutes more.

Remove from oven and allow to stand for 30 minutes before serving. Remove sides of springform pan. The pan and pie will be very hot.

Pure Paragon Beef Stew

PREP TIME: 10 MINUTES | COOK TIME: 2 HOURS | YIELD: 8 SERVINGS

In his famous song about Gaston, LeFou sings, "There's no one in town half as manly. Perfect, a pure paragon." Gaston, not one to be humble, agrees heartily. "You can ask any Tom, Dick, or Stanley," LeFou continues, "and they'll tell you whose team they'd prefer to be on." This beef stew is a pure paragon, just like Gaston believes he is. As the sauce simmers and thickens to a thick and flavorful gravy, it beckons sopping up all the goodness with chunks of bread as thick as Gaston's biceps.

½ cup all-purpose flour

1 teaspoon salt, plus more
  to taste

1 teaspoon black pepper,
  plus more to taste

2 pounds stew beef, cut into
  bite-size pieces

3 tablespoons neutral
  cooking oil

2 large yellow onions,
  chopped

4 russet potatoes, peeled
  and chopped into bite-
  size pieces

2 cups full-bodied red wine

12 cups beef broth

4 bay leaves

2 tablespoons chopped
  fresh thyme or
  2 teaspoons dried thyme

6 large carrots, peeled and
  chopped into bite-size
  pieces

In a medium bowl, combine the flour, salt, and pepper. Dredge the beef pieces in the flour to coat well, then shake off excess.

In a large stockpot over medium heat, heat 1 tablespoon of the oil. Add half the beef, and brown on all sides, about 6 minutes. Remove beef to a plate. Add another tablespoon of oil and repeat. Remove that to a plate.

Add the last tablespoon of oil and the onions to the pot. Cook onions until golden, about 10 minutes. Add the beef, potatoes, red wine, broth, bay leaves, and thyme. Simmer for 1 hour on medium-low heat.

Add the carrots, and simmer another 45 minutes. Remove and discard the bay leaves before serving.

Friends on the Other Side Gumbo

PREP TIME: 15 MINUTES | COOK TIME: 1 HOUR 15 MINUTES | YIELD: 8 TO 10 SERVINGS

When Dr. Facilier brings Prince Naveen and Lawrence into his Voodoo Emporium, he explains to them where his power comes from. "I can read your future, I can change it around some too, I look deep into your heart and soul, make your wildest dreams come true," he says. "I got voodoo, I got hoodoo, I got things I ain't even tried, and I've got friends on the other side."

This gumbo, inspired by the incomparable New Orleans stew, is modified with ingredients that can be found anywhere. If you can't find spicy andouille sausage, use chorizo, and bump up the cayenne pepper a bit.

1 cup (2 sticks) butter

½ cup flour

12 ounces andouille sausage, sliced thin

1 large yellow onion, diced

1 large green bell pepper, diced

2 large stalks celery, diced

4 cloves garlic, minced

One 28-ounce can crushed tomatoes

One 16-ounce package frozen okra, thawed

1 dried bay leaf

1 teaspoon dried thyme

1 teaspoon dried basil

1 teaspoon smoked paprika

1 teaspoon cayenne pepper

1 teaspoon salt

½ teaspoon black pepper

4 cups vegetable stock

1½ pounds shrimp, peeled and deveined

Hot cooked rice

Make the roux. Add the butter and flour to a large stockpot. Cook over medium heat, stirring almost constantly, until the mixture is a rich brown color, about 15 minutes. (If you accidentally burn the roux, start over. Burnt roux will make the gumbo bitter.)

Add the sausage, and cook, stirring frequently, until sausage starts to brown, about 5 minutes.

Add the onion, bell pepper, celery, and garlic. Cook, stirring frequently, until vegetables are tender, 8 to 10 minutes.

Add the tomatoes, okra, herbs, and seasonings. Stir to combine and cook another 5 minutes.

Add the stock and simmer about 30 minutes. Add the shrimp and cook 5 minutes. Remove from heat. Serve gumbo over hot cooked rice.

Fish Dinner

PREP TIME: 10 MINUTES | COOK TIME: 50 MINUTES | YIELD: 6 TO 8 SERVINGS

While Tamatoa sings about how "I've always been shiny" and tries to steal the heart of the ocean from Moana, he takes a quick break from his song to grab and eat some fish. "Mmm, fish dinner!" This fish dinner isn't exactly what that shiny crab eats, but it's a New England-style seafood pie that will warm you up on a cold night or after a chilly dip in the ocean. Using milk in place of the cream will make this dish lighter, but the sauce won't be as thick.

2 medium Yukon gold potatoes, peeled and diced

2 tablespoons olive oil

1 large onion, diced

3 garlic cloves, minced

½ a large leek, white and tender green parts only, sliced into thin rounds

1 large stalk celery, diced

½ pound shrimp, peeled and deveined

½ pound whitefish, cut into small pieces

½ pound bay scallops

Juice of 1 lemon

3 tablespoons butter

3 tablespoons all-purpose flour

2 cups cream or milk

2 tablespoons fresh dill

2 tablespoons fresh parsley

1 tablespoon Dijon mustard

½ cup frozen or fresh peas

Salt and pepper to taste

1 sheet of frozen puff pastry, thawed

1 egg, beaten

In a medium saucepan over high heat, boil the potatoes in water to cover until potatoes begin to get tender, about 10 minutes. Drain and set aside.

Preheat oven to 400°F.

In a large sauté pan over medium heat, heat the olive oil, then sauté the onion, garlic, leek, celery, and potatoes until beginning to soften, about 5 minutes. Add the seafood and lemon juice. Cook 5 minutes.

While seafood is cooking, prepare the sauce. In a medium saucepan over medium heat, melt the butter, then whisk in the flour, and slowly whisk in the cream. Stir until sauce thickens, about 3 minutes.

Add the sauce to the seafood, along with the dill, parsley, Dijon mustard, and peas. Season to taste with salt and pepper. Unroll the puff pastry and roll into a 9-by-13-inch rectangle. Use the back of a spoon to indent the entire surface of the pastry in a scale pattern.

Transfer filling to a 9-by-13-inch baking dish. Top with puff pastry. Brush with the beaten egg, then bake until golden, about 30 minutes.

NUTRITIOUS TIP: Feel free to swap out any of the seafood for another that you prefer, like heart-healthy salmon.

Hazelnut Soup

PREP TIME: 10 MINUTES | COOK TIME: 1 HOUR 45 MINUTES | YIELD: 6 SERVINGS

Mother Gothel tries her best to keep Rapunzel happy while locked away in the tower. "I brought back parsnips," Mother Gothel says to the imprisoned princess at the tower window. "I'm going to make hazelnut soup for dinner. Surprise!" That soup may not have been enough to keep Rapunzel in her tower, but this soup is a delicious surprise.

¾ cup raw hazelnuts, shelled and skins removed, divided, plus more for garnish

1 medium acorn squash

3 tablespoons olive oil, divided

2 large shallots, thinly sliced

1 pound parsnips, chopped

2 Granny Smith apples, cored and chopped, plus more for garnish

6 cups vegetable stock

1 tablespoon chopped fresh thyme, plus more for garnish

Preheat the oven to 275°F. Spread ¼ cup hazelnuts on a rimmed baking sheet and bake about 25 minutes. Remove from oven and allow to cool. Chop the hazelnuts.

Increase oven temperature to 375°F. Cut the acorn squash in half, and scoop out the seeds and pith. Drizzle cut sides with 1½ tablespoons olive oil. Place squash in a baking dish, cut sides down, and bake until tender, 35 to 40 minutes. Remove from oven. When cool enough to handle, scoop out the flesh and discard the rind.

In a large stockpot over medium heat, heat the remaining olive oil. Add shallots and cook until tender, about 5 minutes. Add parsnips, apples, and remaining ½ cup hazelnuts; continue to cook 5 minutes.

Add the vegetable stock, thyme, and squash. Cook for about 30 minutes, until vegetables are tender. Remove from heat.

Puree soup using an immersion blender in the pot, or in batches using a blender. Garnish with chopped toasted hazelnuts, thin slices of green apple, and additional thyme.

NUTRITIOUS TIP: This healthy vegan soup is full of protein. If you can't find hazelnuts, substitute cashews.

Olympus Moussaka

PREP TIME: 1 HOUR | COOK TIME: 1 HOUR 30 MINUTES | BAKE TIME: 1 HOUR | YIELD: 10 SERVINGS

Hades, the fast-talking, short-tempered god of the underworld, isn't impressed by the arrival of his brother Zeus' son, Hercules. "How sentimental," he sneers. "You know, I haven't been this choked up since I got a chunk of moussaka stuck in my throat."

This vegetarian moussaka is the kind of dish that will certainly draw cheers from the crowd. It's hearty enough to satisfy meat-lovers, and full of naturally occurring plant protein, with layers of vegetables and a creamy béchamel sauce. Ample ingredients ensure a hearty dish, with plenty for leftovers.

2 small eggplants

½ cup olive oil, divided

1 teaspoon salt

1 teaspoon pepper

6 cloves garlic, minced

4 medium zucchini

1 medium yellow onion, diced

2 large stalks celery, diced

2 large carrots, diced

16 ounces cremini mushrooms, sliced

1 tablespoon chopped fresh oregano

½ teaspoon ground cinnamon

2 cups cooked lentils

One 14.5-ounce can crushed tomatoes

½ teaspoon cayenne pepper

1 cup crumbled feta cheese

3 tablespoons butter

3 tablespoons all-purpose flour

3 cups milk

1 teaspoon nutmeg

4 egg yolks, beaten

1 cup grated Parmesan cheese, divided

Peel the eggplants and cut into ¼-inch-thick slices lengthwise. Soak in a large bowl of salted water at least 30 minutes to draw out bitterness. Drain and pat dry.

Preheat oven to 450°F. On two baking sheets, arrange eggplant slices. Drizzle with 3 tablespoons olive oil and a pinch of salt and pepper. Bake for 8 minutes, then flip and bake another 8 minutes. Remove from oven, transfer eggplant slices to a platter, cover, and set aside.

Slice the zucchini lengthwise. On the same baking sheets, lay out the zucchini slices. Drizzle with 3 tablespoons olive oil and a pinch of salt and pepper. Bake for 5 minutes, then flip and bake another 5 minutes. Remove from oven and set aside. Reduce oven temperature to 400°F.

In a large skillet over medium heat, heat the remaining 2 tablespoons olive oil. Add the garlic, onion, celery, and carrots. Cook until softened, about 10 minutes. Add the mushrooms, oregano, and cinnamon; cook another 10 minutes. Add the lentils, tomatoes, and cayenne pepper; cook 5 minutes more to incorporate flavors.

In a large baking dish, evenly layer half the eggplant slices. Repeat with half the zucchini slices. Top with the lentil mixture, then the feta. Layer remaining zucchini then remaining eggplant.

Prepare the béchamel sauce. In a medium saucepan over medium heat, melt the butter and flour. Whisk until the flour mixture is golden brown, about 5 minutes. Slowly whisk in the milk, a little at a time, then add the nutmeg. Slowly whisk in the egg yolks, stirring constantly. Add ½ cup Parmesan, 1 teaspoon salt, and 1 teaspoon pepper. Cook for 3 minutes more at a low simmer to thicken.

Pour béchamel over top of vegetables in dish. Top with remaining Parmesan. Bake 30 minutes. Remove from the oven and let stand at least 15 minutes.

Chicken Soup for Sick Dragons

PREP TIME: 10 MINUTES | COOK TIME: 45 MINUTES | YIELD: 8 SERVINGS

At the end of their Wizards Duel, Madam Mim is sure she's won. She turns into a giant purple dragon—breaking her own rule against transforming into make-believe things—and grabs Merlin, who's currently a mouse, in her claws. "I win!" she exclaims. "I win!" Then all of a sudden, Merlin disappears.

"I'm a germ, a rare disease. I'm called malignalitaloptereosis, and you caught me, Mim!," Merlin says. "First you break out into spots, followed by hot and cold flashes, then violent sneezing."

Merlin prescribes bed rest and lots of sunshine for Mim, but any mom knows that chicken soup makes anyone who's under the weather feel better. This soup has bone broth, known for its healing properties, and bow tie pasta to evoke Mim's dragon wings. Here's the secret, though: You don't have to be sick to enjoy this classic soup. Even sweater weather will do.

2 tablespoons olive oil

3 medium onions, diced

4 cloves garlic, minced

4 large carrots, diced

4 large celery stalks, diced

1 teaspoon salt

1 teaspoon pepper

2 tablespoons dried dill

12 cups chicken stock

4 cups chicken bone broth

4 cups shredded cooked
   chicken

1½ cups bow tie pasta

In a large stockpot over medium heat, heat the olive oil, then add the onions and garlic. Cook until the onions are translucent, about 10 minutes. Add the carrots and celery, and cook another 10 minutes.

Add the salt, pepper, dill, stock, broth, and chicken. Bring to a simmer and cook for 10 minutes. Add the pasta and simmer another 10 minutes. Serve hot, to dragons or people.

Codfish and Chips

PREP TIME: 20 MINUTES | COOK TIME: 20 MINUTES | YIELD: 4 SERVINGS

Captain Hook is determined to exact his revenge against the mischievous Peter Pan. But no matter how hard he tries, Hook just can't get the upper hand with the crafty leader of the Lost Boys and that pesky Tick-Tock Crocodile.

"I'll get you for this, Pan!" the Captain shouts! "If it's the last thing I do!" But when Pan has Hook tied up on the Jolly Roger and makes the captain shout "I'm a codfiiiish!," the captain is further defeated.

This fish and chips recipe, inspired by a classic combo, is flaky white codfish and crispy chips at its best. Sprinkle with malt vinegar and salt, as the Brits do, or serve with tartar sauce for dipping.

FOR THE CHIPS
2 pounds large russet potatoes

Salt to taste

Neutral cooking oil

FOR THE CODFISH
2 pounds cod

1½ cups flour

1½ tablespoons cornstarch

1½ teaspoons baking powder

8 to 10 ounces club soda

Neutral cooking oil

Prepare the potatoes. Rinse well and peel, if desired. Cut each potato into long, thin strips. The skinnier the chips are, the crisper they'll be. Soak the chips in cold water at least 2 hours or overnight.

Prepare the fish. Cut the cod into 4 pieces of equal size and pat dry.

In a large mixing bowl, combine the dry ingredients. Add the club soda to make a thick batter that is just thin enough that most of the excess batter will drip off the fish.

Fill a large pot with 4 inches of cooking oil; heat over medium-high until very hot, about 375°F if using a thermometer. (Or, if a sprinkle of water on the oil sizzles, it is hot enough to begin cooking.)

Dip each piece of cod into the batter, then place in the hot oil so no pieces touch. Cook about 3 minutes per side, until golden brown. Remove to a plate lined with paper towels. Cover to keep warm.

Drain the potatoes, and dry with a paper towel.

In the same large pot with 4 inches of oil, heat over medium-high until very hot (about 375°F). Fry potatoes in batches until golden brown, then remove to paper towels to drain. Season with salt. Serve with the fish.

Cakes & Pies

Bioluminescent Diversion

Unbirthday Cake

Molten Lava Cakes

Spotted Dog Pudding Cake With Vanilla Custard

Skillet Berry Pie

Voodoo Top Hat Cake

Mistress of All Evil Trifle

Snake Pie

Bioluminescent Diversion

Tamatoa's bright purple shell is adorned with as many shiny things as it can possibly hold, but he always wants more—and he'd definitely be after this vivid treat if he could. This Bundt cake is vivid inside, and has a multicolor glaze to create a diversion as attention-grabbing as the sinister crab himself. If you would rather have a vanilla cake than a coconut one, just add additional vanilla extract instead of using coconut extract, and omit the shredded coconut from the recipe.

FOR THE CAKE

- 3 cups all-purpose flour
- 3 tablespoons cornstarch
- 1½ teaspoons baking powder
- 1½ teaspoons kosher salt
- 1½ cups (3 sticks) salted butter, at room temperature
- 3 cups granulated sugar
- 1 tablespoon vanilla extract
- 1 tablespoon coconut extract
- 4 large eggs
- 1 cup whole milk
- 1 cup sweetened shredded coconut, plus more for sprinkling on top, if desired
- 4 bright (neon if possible) colors of food coloring
- Nonstick cooking spray

FOR THE GLAZE

- 3 cups powdered sugar
- 6 tablespoons whole milk
- ½ teaspoon pure vanilla extract
- ½ teaspoon coconut extract
- 4 bright (neon if possible) colors of food coloring

Prepare the cake. Preheat oven to 350°F. In a large mixing bowl, combine the flour, cornstarch, baking powder, and salt.

In the bowl of a stand mixer, beat together the butter and sugar until light and fluffy, about 2 minutes. Add the vanilla and coconut extracts, then the eggs one at a time, beating well after each addition.

Add half the dry ingredients to the wet ingredients, beating just until combined. Pour in milk and coconut, and mix until fully incorporated. Add remaining dry ingredients and mix until just combined.

Divide the batter equally among four small mixing bowls. Add a small amount of one food coloring to each bowl, stirring to achieve the desired color.

Spray a 12-cup Bundt pan with cooking spray. Alternately drop batter from each of the four bowls into the pan. Bake until a toothpick inserted into the cake center comes out clean, 55 to 60 minutes. Let cool in pan 10 minutes, then invert onto a cooling rack or platter to cool completely.

Prepare the glaze. In a small saucepan over medium heat, whisk together the powdered sugar, milk, and vanilla. Stir for 2 minutes. Remove from heat, and divide among four small mixing bowls. Starting with the darkest color, add a small amount of food coloring to a bowl, mixing to achieve desired color. Immediately drizzle glaze on cake. Repeat with remaining three colors, working quickly because the icing begins to set as soon as it is removed from the heat. Sprinkle with shredded coconut, if desired. Let set completely before serving, if you can resist.

Unbirthday Cake

PREP TIME: 30 MINUTES | COOK TIME: 30 MINUTES | YIELD: 12 SERVINGS

When the Mad Hatter is called to testify in the trial against Alice, he reports that he has spent the day having tea. "Today, you know, is my unbirthday," he explains.

"Why, my dear, today is your unbirthday too!" the King of Hearts says to his wife. "It is?" the Queen of Hearts responds. Then the whole courtroom erupts in a round of "A Very Merry Unbirthday to You" for the Queen and presents her with a cake, distracting her, for the moment, from beheadings.

This rich red velvet cake, crowned with roses and symbols for playing card suits, is suitable for a queen, a birthday, unbirthday, or any occasion.

FOR THE CAKE

1 cup vegetable oil

1 cup buttermilk

3 large eggs

1 tablespoon red food coloring

1 teaspoon white vinegar

1 teaspoon vanilla extract

2½ cups all-purpose flour

1½ cups sugar

1 teaspoon baking soda

1 teaspoon salt

1 tablespoon cocoa powder

Nonstick cooking spray

FOR THE FROSTING

1 pound cream cheese, at room temperature

4 cups confectioners sugar

1 cup (2 sticks) butter, at room temperature

1 teaspoon vanilla extract

FOR THE DECORATIONS

1½ cups milk chocolate chips

2 ounces black fondant

Premade red icing roses

Prepare the cake. Preheat oven to 350°F.

In the bowl of a stand mixer, combine the vegetable oil, buttermilk, eggs, food coloring, vinegar, and vanilla. Mix until combined. Add the flour, sugar, baking soda, salt, and cocoa powder. Beat on medium for 2 minutes, until smooth.

Spray two 9-inch round cake pans with cooking spray. Divide the batter evenly between the pans, then tap them on the counter to remove bubbles from the batter. Bake until a knife inserted in the center of each cake comes out clean, about 28 minutes.

Remove from oven, and let cool briefly in pans. Then turn out onto a wire rack to cool completely.

While cakes cool, prepare the frosting. Combine all ingredients in the bowl of a stand mixer, and beat on medium-high until smooth, about 4 minutes. Chill until ready to use.

continued on page 81

continued from page 79

When the cakes are completely cooled, level the tops with a serrated knife to flatten. Discard cake scraps. Place one cake, cut side up, on a serving platter. Spread a generous layer of frosting on the top, then add the second cake, cut side down. Spread remaining frosting on top and sides of cake until smooth. Press chocolate chips evenly into the sides of the cake. Refrigerate 30 minutes to set.

While cake is chilling, prepare the fondant playing card suits. Roll out the fondant into a thin layer, at most ⅛-inch thickness. Using a sharp paring knife, cut out a heart, club, spade, and diamond. Carefully add them to the top of the cake, then add premade red icing roses.

Molten Lava Cakes

PREP TIME: 20 MINUTES | BAKE TIME: 17 MINUTES | YIELD: 4 SERVINGS

The nefarious Chernabog presides over his kingdom of Bald Mountain, a dark crag rising into the sky. Winged beasties and fire sprites dance around him as the sky glowers. This is the land of the night, and towering above it, stands a molten mountain filled with liquid fire.

These rich and chocolatey Molten Lava Cakes are not nearly as scary as Chernabog. The "molten lava" inside is warm and melty gooey chocolate enveloped by cake for an irresistible dessert, made even more luscious with whipped cream or ice cream.

½ cup (1 stick) butter

2 tablespoons bittersweet chocolate chips

6 tablespoons semisweet chocolate chips

1 cup powdered sugar

2 whole eggs plus 3 egg yolks

1 teaspoon vanilla

1 teaspoon espresso powder

½ cup all-purpose flour

Nonstick cooking spray

Whipped cream or ice cream

Preheat oven to 425°F.

In a medium mixing bowl, add the butter and chocolate chips. Set bowl in a saucepan of water, bottom of bowl above water level. Over low heat, stir chocolate just until melted. Remove bowl from pan of water.

Whisk in the sugar until combined, then add the whole eggs and yolks, vanilla, espresso powder, and flour, stirring well between after each addition.

Spray four 6-ounce ramekins with cooking spray, then divide the batter evenly among dishes.

Bake for 15 to 17 minutes, until edges are set and centers remain soft.

Remove from oven and let stand 5 minutes. Serve with whipped cream or ice cream.

Spotted Dog Pudding Cake With Vanilla Custard

PREP TIME: 20 MINUTES | COOK TIME: 1 HOUR 30 MINUTES | YIELD: 8 SERVINGS

Cruella De Vil, who searches for Pongo and Perdita's spotted dalmatian pups, probably should have just settled for this delicious dessert instead. Sometimes called Spotted Dick or Railway Cake, Spotted Dog is a traditional British pudding that is steamed in a big pot of simmering water, then served with vanilla custard. Pudding molds are easy and inexpensive to purchase online, or you can make do with a Bundt pan wrapped tightly in aluminum foil, then tied with kitchen twine. The result looks and cuts like a cake, but it's lighter, mildly sweet, and totally unforgettable.

FOR THE PUDDING

½ cup (1 stick) butter, cut into chunks

2 cups all-purpose flour

2 teaspoons baking powder

¼ teaspoon salt

1 cup granulated sugar

1 cup milk

1 tablespoon vanilla extract

Zest of 1 large lemon

Zest of 1 orange

1 cup dried currants (use golden raisins or dried blueberries if you can't find currants)

Nonstick cooking spray

FOR THE VANILLA CUSTARD

4 egg yolks

⅓ cup granulated sugar

1 tablespoon vanilla bean paste

1 cup milk

1 cup heavy cream

Prepare the pudding. Fill a large stockpot halfway with water. In the bottom of the pot, place something to hold the pudding mold above the bottom of the pot. (A small cooling rack works best, or you could use metal cookie cutters or an inverted ovenproof bowl.)

In the bowl of a food processor, pulse the butter, flour, baking powder, salt, and sugar until the mixture resembles sand.

In a large mixing bowl, combine the milk, vanilla, and zest. Add the butter mixture, and stir until combined. Stir in the currants.

Liberally spray the inside of the pudding mold with cooking spray, then pour in the batter. Seal the top with the lid. If using a Bundt pan and foil, tightly fasten the foil to the pan with twine to make as air- and water-tight as possible.

Place the pudding mold on the rack in the pot. If necessary, adjust the water level in the pot to rise just to halfway up the mold. Cover the pot and bring water to a simmer over medium heat. Cook undisturbed for 1 hour 30 minutes. Carefully remove the pudding mold from the water—there will be a lot of steam. Allow to cool for 10 minutes in the mold.

While the pudding is setting, prepare the vanilla custard. In a medium mixing bowl, combine the egg yolks, sugar, and vanilla paste.

In a medium saucepan over medium heat, combine the milk and cream. Heat until the mixture just starts to simmer. (Do not allow it to boil or it will curdle.) Pour about ½ cup of the warm liquid into bowl with egg yolks, whisking quickly to prevent egg mixture from cooking. Whisk for 1 minute to temper the egg yolk mixture. Slowly whisk the contents of the bowl back into the saucepan. Simmer 3 to 4 minutes, until the custard has thickened and on the verge of boiling. (Caution: Prevent custard from boiling, which causes curdling and unappealing lumps.)

Invert the mold onto a plate. Slice the cake, then top generously with custard.

Skillet Berry Pie

PREP TIME: 15 MINUTES | COOK TIME: 45 MINUTES | YIELD: 6 SERVINGS

"It's a scary world out there," Mother Gothel sings as Rapunzel asks to leave the tower. "Something will go wrong, I swear. Ruffians, thugs, poison ivy, quicksand, cannibals and snakes, the plague," she sings, flipping a doll in a skillet. Despite Mother Gothel's dire warnings, Rapunzel leaves her tower, taking the skillet with her for protection.

After you try this berry pie, you might become attached to your skillet too—for a different reason. Simple to prepare and a showstopper at the table, this Skillet Berry Pie might be added to your regular rotation.

FOR THE PIE FILLING

1½ cups sugar

1 teaspoon cinnamon

¼ cup cornstarch

3 pints of berries, such as blueberries, blackberries, raspberries, and/or strawberries

Juice of 1 lemon

Nonstick cooking spray

FOR THE STREUSEL TOPPING

1 cup flour

1 cup sugar

2 teaspoons cinnamon

1 teaspoon nutmeg

½ cup (1 stick) butter, at room temperature

Ice cream or whipped cream (optional)

Preheat oven to 400°F.

Prepare the filling. In a large mixing bowl, combine the sugar, cinnamon, and cornstarch. Stir, then add the berries and lemon juice.

Spray a medium cast-iron (or ovenproof) skillet with cooking spray. Over medium-low heat, add the berry mixture. Cook about 5 minutes, until berries are coated.

Prepare the streusel topping. In a medium bowl, combine the flour, sugar, and spices. Mix in the butter until topping is crumbly.

Pour the topping over the berries, but do not mix. Bake for 45 minutes, until the streusel is golden brown. Let stand 30 minutes before serving. Serve with ice cream or whipped cream, if desired.

Voodoo Top Hat Cake

PREP TIME: 30 MINUTES | COOK TIME: 25 MINUTES | YIELD: 12 SERVINGS

Dr. Facilier, purveyor of "tarot readings, charms, potions, dreams made real," attempts to use his voodoo and hoodoo powers to take over New Orleans and bend the city to his will. His distinctive top hat hovers over the crowd, its skull and crossbones leering down at the people he would control. This dense cake is a bold statement in favor of dessert, not voodoo power.

FOR THE CAKE

4 eggs

1 cup buttermilk

¼ cup vegetable oil

1 teaspoon vanilla extract

2 cups all-purpose flour

2 cups granulated sugar

1 cup cocoa powder

2 teaspoons baking soda

1 teaspoon baking powder

1 teaspoon salt

Nonstick cooking spray

FOR THE BUTTERCREAM FROSTING

¾ cup (1½ sticks) butter, softened

6 cups confectioners sugar

1 teaspoon almond extract

3 egg whites

FOR THE DECORATION

One 24-ounce package black fondant

One 4-ounce package white fondant

One 4-ounce package red fondant

1 purple feather

Preheat oven to 350°F.

Prepare the cake. In the bowl of a stand mixer, combine the eggs, buttermilk, oil, and vanilla; mix on low to combine. In a medium mixing bowl, combine the flour, sugar, cocoa powder, baking soda, baking powder, and salt. Slowly add the dry mix to the liquids, then beat on medium until smooth.

Spray three 6-inch round cake pans with cooking spray. Divide the batter evenly among the pans. (If necessary to bake cakes in batches, refrigerate batter until ready to fill pans.)

Bake until a knife inserted in center of cakes comes out clean, about 25 minutes. Allow cakes to rest, about 10 minutes. Turn out onto a wire rack to cool before frosting, about 2 hours.

Prepare the frosting. In the bowl of a stand mixer, combine all ingredients and beat on medium speed until thoroughly combined, about 3 minutes.

Decorate the cake. Place one cake on a black serving platter, then apply a generous layer of buttercream. Repeat with two remaining cakes. When all three are in place, frost cake with buttercream.

Prepare the fondant. Knead a softball-size amount of black fondant until pliable. Roll into a 16-inch circle, then center on top of the cake and drape. Gently stretch fondant to cover the entire cake.

Knead a golf-ball-size amount of white fondant until pliable. Roll into a 6-inch circle, then cut out a skull-and-crossbones pattern. Use a small amount of frosting to attach the shape to the center of the cake.

Knead a tennis-ball-size amount of red fondant until pliable. Roll to a 2-by-18-inch band, then attach to hat with a small amount of frosting. Tuck the purple feather into the hatband.

Mistress of All Evil Trifle

PREP TIME: 30 MINUTES | COOK TIME: 20 MINUTES | YIELD: 10 SERVINGS

For 16 years, Maleficent waits and watches from the Forbidden Mountains to carry out her evil plan for Princess Aurora. When the princess returns to the castle, Maleficent lures Aurora up a turret to a spinning wheel. The princess pricks her finger and immediately falls under Maleficent's spell. "You poor, simple fools!" she gloats over the fairies, laughing her evil laugh. "Thinking you could defeat me—me, the Mistress of All Evil!"

This wickedly decadent trifle, richly layered with homemade pistachio pudding and witchy purple cream, makes a devilishly delicious impression. The chocolate cake is baked in a large baking dish at 325°F about 35 minutes for easy crumbling to layer in tall trifle dishes.

FOR THE PUDDING
1½ cups shelled pistachios

3 tablespoons cornstarch

½ teaspoon salt

4 egg yolks

2 cups heavy cream

3 cups milk

1 cup granulated sugar

¼ cup butter

1½ teaspoons vanilla extract

FOR THE WHIPPED CREAM
2 teaspoons plain gelatin

3 scant tablespoons water

3 cups heavy cream

Purple food coloring

1 teaspoon vanilla extract

¼ cup confectioners sugar

FOR THE TRIFLE
One 15.25-ounce box chocolate cake mix, baked according to package directions and cut into small pieces

Green and purple fancy sprinkles

Place a stand mixer bowl in the freezer to chill. Prepare the pudding. In the bowl of a food processor, process the pistachios until finely ground, about 4 minutes. Remove to a medium mixing bowl, and add the cornstarch and salt. In another mixing bowl, whisk together the egg yolks and cream. Slowly whisk the nut mixture into the liquid.

In a large saucepan over medium heat, add the milk and sugar. Bring to a simmer, with bubbles just rising at the edges of the pan.

Temper the cream mixture with half the liquid in the pan, whisking quickly to prevent curdling or cooking. Once combined, pour the mixture back into the saucepan.

Bring to a boil, whisking constantly and cooking for 3 minutes, until very thick. Remove from heat, then add the butter and vanilla. Sir until butter is melted, then pour into a bowl. Cover with plastic wrap touching surface of pudding (to prevent skin from forming). Chill pudding at least 4 hours.

Prepare the whipped cream. In a small heatproof bowl, combine the gelatin and water. Let stand 5 minutes. Microwave for 10 seconds for gelatin to liquefy; whisk until smooth.

In the chilled stand mixer bowl, add the cream, food coloring, and vanilla. Whip on medium-high, shaking the sugar into the mixer a bit at a time. When whipped cream forms soft peaks, slowly pour in liquid gelatin. Beat 1 minute more, until stiff peaks form. Chill until using.

Prepare the trifle. In ten 12-ounce trifle glasses, layer pudding, chocolate cake pieces, and whipped cream. Repeat layers. Top with sprinkles, and refrigerate until serving.

Snake Pie

PREP TIME: 30 MINUTES | COOK TIME: 30 MINUTES | YIELD: 10 SERVINGS

The enormous python Kaa is as beguiling as he is terrifying, thanks to his powers of persuasion. He is one of the most dangerous animals lurking in the jungle and uses his hypnotizing eyes to ensnare prey into his coils. "Say now, what have we here?" he says when he first discovers Mowgli. "A man cub. A delicioussssssss man cub."

You'll want to get into the coils of this delicious almond-orange pastry, shaped like a snake and inspired by the North African dessert called M'hanncha, which translates to snake pie. Working with phyllo is tricky because it tears easily, but it's also easy to repair with patches of dough affixed with melted butter. You'll be richly rewarded for your efforts: This dessert is even better for breakfast the next morning.

FOR THE FILLING

3 cups raw almonds

¾ cup confectioners sugar

½ teaspoon ground cinnamon

¼ teaspoon ground cardamom

¾ cup (1½ sticks) unsalted butter, melted

2 egg yolks, beaten

Juice of 1 medium orange

Zest of 1 medium orange

1 teaspoon vanilla extract

FOR THE CAKE

12 sheets phyllo dough, thawed if frozen

¾ cup (1½ sticks) unsalted butter, melted

2 egg yolks, beaten

1 tablespoon water

1 teaspoon cinnamon

¼ cup confectioners sugar

¼ cup sliced almonds

Prepare the filling. In a food processor, combine the almonds, sugar, cinnamon, and cardamom; grind into meal, about 1 minute. Add the butter and egg yolks, and pulse to blend. Add the orange juice, orange zest, and vanilla, and pulse once more to combine.

Remove the filling to a bowl, then cover and refrigerate at least 30 minutes.

Prepare the Cake. Preheat oven to 350°F. Fold each sheet of phyllo lengthwise into thirds. Quickly brush all with melted butter. Place about 3 tablespoons of filling at one wide end of the sheet, and spread evenly across the bottom inch. Starting with the filling end, roll tightly and seal the end with melted butter. Form a coil by attaching dough sections, using more phyllo and melted butter to repair any tears in the fragile dough. Transfer to a baking sheet lined with parchment paper.

Combine the egg, water, and cinnamon, then brush the top of the pie with the mixture. Bake until golden brown, about 30 minutes. Allow to cool, then sprinkle with confectioners sugar and almonds.

Cookies & Sweets

Poison Apples

Bald Mountain Cookies

Temper, Temper Hearts

Bowl of Worms Pudding

Hypnotizing Snake Staffs

Tiger Tails

Evil Cream Horns

Poison Apples

PREP TIME: 15 MINUTES | COOK TIME: 60 MINUTES | YIELD: 6 SERVINGS

The Queen persuades Snow White to eat a poison apple, and a single bite is all it takes for the young princess to succumb to the sinister queen's plans.

You won't be able to stop at just a taste of these sweet and savory baked apples with "poison" green caramel sauce. Make sure you select apples that will stand upright in a pan while baking.

FOR THE BAKED APPLES

6 firm apples, like Granny Smith or Honeycrisp

½ cup (1 stick) butter, softened

1 cup light brown sugar

1½ teaspoons cinnamon

1 teaspoon ground ginger

½ cup chopped pecans

1½ cups apple cider

FOR THE "POISON" CARAMEL SAUCE

½ cup (1 stick) butter, softened

1 cup light brown sugar

½ cup heavy cream

1 teaspoon vanilla extract

¼ teaspoon salt

Green gel paste

Prepare the apples. Preheat oven to 375°F. Core each apple with a coring tool or with a paring knife and spoon. Make the opening in each apple about 1¼ inches wide, leaving the bottom intact to hold the filling.

In a medium mixing bowl, combine the butter, sugar, cinnamon, ginger, and pecans. Spoon the filling equally into each apple, then stand the apples in a medium baking dish. Pour the apple cider into the baking dish to coat the bottom—you may need slightly more or less depending on size of pan.

Bake until tender, 50 to 60 minutes, depending on size of apples.

Prepare the caramel sauce. In a small saucepan over medium-high heat, bring the butter, sugar, and cream to a boil. Immediately reduce to a simmer and cook, stirring often, about 5 minutes, until the caramel starts to thicken.

Remove from the heat, then stir in the vanilla, salt, and enough food coloring to turn the sauce green.

Place each apple in an individual serving bowl, then spoon the sauce over the top. Serve while hot.

NUTRITIOUS TIP: Apples contain lots of fiber, which aids digestion. Keeping the skin on maximizes fiber content.

Bald Mountain Cookies

PREP TIME: 10 MINUTES | COOK TIME: 15 MINUTES | YIELD: 12 COOKIES

Atop the foreboding Bald Mountain, evil lurks. Chernabog casts darkness over the village below, summoning fire and demons.

These chocolate haystack cookies evoke the darkness of Bald Mountain, with two red eyes in each one to create the illusion of the beast himself.

½ cup semisweet chocolate chips

3 egg whites

¼ cup cocoa powder

¾ cup granulated sugar

½ teaspoon salt

1½ teaspoons vanilla extract

2½ cups sweetened shredded coconut

24 pieces red cinnamon candy

In a small glass bowl, microwave the chocolate chips for 30 seconds. Stir, then microwave another 30 seconds. Stir until totally smooth, then set aside to cool to room temperature.

In the bowl of a stand mixer, beat the egg whites until frothy yet soft. Slowly add in the cocoa powder, sugar, salt, and vanilla.

Remove the bowl from the mixer, and stir in the coconut and cooled chocolate by hand. Cover and refrigerate for 1 hour.

Preheat oven to 325°F. Line a cookie sheet with parchment paper. Drop 12 even spoonfuls of batter onto the sheet, then shape them into mountain shapes by hand. Add two red candies to each. Freeze for 10 minutes to retain shape, then bake for 13 to 15 minutes. Remove from the oven and cool.

Temper, Temper Hearts

PREP TIME: 45 MINUTES | COOK TIME: 8 MINUTES PER BATCH | YIELD: 4 DOZEN COOKIES

The Queen of Hearts is *always* losing her temper, and then shouting hot-headed things like "SILENCE!" and, of course, "OFF WITH HER HEAD!"

These red heart sugar cookies display some of the iconic sayings of the queen and her husband, the King of Hearts, in bold white icing. Decorate with whatever phrases and shapes, like suits from playing cards or roses. Find meringue powder at a local crafts or baking store, or find powdered egg white replacement at a grocery store.

FOR THE COOKIES

2½ cups flour, plus additional for rolling

1 teaspoon baking powder

½ teaspoon baking soda

½ teaspoon salt

1 cup (2 sticks) butter, softened

1 cup granulated sugar

1 egg

1½ teaspoons vanilla extract

2 teaspoons red food coloring

FOR THE ICING

4 cups confectioners sugar

3 tablespoons meringue powder

6 tablespoons water

In a medium bowl, combine the flour, baking powder, baking soda, and salt; set aside.

In the bowl of a stand mixer, beat the butter and sugar until fluffy, about 3 minutes. Add the egg, vanilla, and food coloring, and beat another 1 minute.

Slowly add the flour mixture and mix until fully combined. Remove from the mixer; divide the dough in half. Wrap each half in plastic wrap, and refrigerate at least 1 hour.

Preheat oven to 350°F. Working with one dough half at a time and keeping remaining dough refrigerated, roll out dough on a floured work surface to a ⅛-inch thickness. Using a heart-shape cookie cutter, cut out as many cookies as you can. Keep the scraps to roll into the next batch. Place cookies on a baking sheet lined with parchment paper, spacing so they do not touch.

Repeat with remaining dough. Bake just until turning golden, about 8 minutes. Remove from oven and allow to cool.

Prepare the icing. In the bowl of a stand mixer, combine the sugar, meringue powder, and water. Mix until combined, about 3 minutes. If the icing seems too thick, add a bit more water.

Transfer the icing to a pastry bag fitted with a small round writing tip. Decorate each cookie as you like with sayings from the Red Queen and Red King, such as "OFF WITH HER HEAD!" and "Temper, Temper, My Sweet." Allow icing to set for 1 hour before serving.

Bowl of Worms Pudding

PREP TIME: 10 MINUTES | COOK TIME: 10 MINUTES | YIELD: 6 SERVINGS

When Hades sets up Hercules to battle a fearsome Hydra, he makes sure to get a snack to enjoy during the show. What else would the resentful god find suitable for such an occasion than a bowl of fresh worms?

   If you aren't the god of the underworld, this Bowl of Worms has more appeal than the one from the movie. Rich chocolate pudding is topped with cookie crumble "dirt" and candy "worms," to enjoy the next time you watch a demigod defeat a mythic monster—or just for dessert after a nice dinner.

½ cup granulated sugar

¼ cup cocoa powder

3 tablespoons cornstarch

¼ teaspoon salt

3 egg yolks

1½ cups heavy cream

2 cups whole milk

1 teaspoon vanilla extract

4 ounces bittersweet chocolate chips

12 chocolate creme-filled cookies, filling removed, or 24 chocolate cookie wafers, crushed

18 gummy worms

In a large saucepan, combine the sugar, cocoa powder, cornstarch, and salt. Whisk in the egg yolks, cream, and milk until combined.

Bring to a simmer over medium-high, and, whisking constantly, cook for 3 minutes or until very thick. Remove from heat, then add the vanilla and chocolate chips. Stir until chocolate is melted, then pour into six serving bowls. Cover surface directly with plastic wrap (to prevent skin from forming), then refrigerate for 1 hour or until chilled.

When ready to serve, divide crushed cookies evenly among the pudding bowls, then top with gummy worms. Serve cold.

Hypnotizing Snake Staffs

PREP TIME: 10 MINUTES | COOK TIME: 30 MINUTES | YIELD: 12 PIECES

Jafar uses the snake eyes on the top of his staff to hypnotize people into doing his dastardly deeds, like making the Sultan order Princess Jasmine to marry the evil sorcerer. These Hypnotizing Snake Staffs are enchanting for another reason: They're so delicious that they're impossible to resist. Just try it. You'll see.

¼ cup (½ stick) butter

1 cup granulated sugar

½ cup light corn syrup

6 ounces evaporated milk

12 long pretzel rods

2 cups milk chocolate chips

Red and gold fancy sprinkles and candy pieces

Prepare the caramel. In a medium saucepan over medium heat, combine the butter, sugar, and corn syrup. Bring to a boil, stirring frequently.

Very slowly pour in the evaporated milk, 1 ounce at a time, stirring constantly for 2 minutes after each addition. Make sure the caramel sauce is boiling the entire time. Cook and stir until the caramel becomes a soft ball. Test the firmness by using a candy thermometer (235°F) or by dropping a bit in cold water and seeing whether it's sturdy enough to mold the caramel in your hands after cooling in the water.

Remove from heat and allow to cool for 5 minutes. Line a work surface or baking sheet with parchment paper. Dip each pretzel two-thirds into the caramel, using a spoon if necessary. Place each on the parchment paper, and allow to cool completely. If caramel coating flattens, gently roll around the pretzel rod.

In a small glass bowl, microwave the chocolate chips for 1 minute. Stir, then microwave another 30 seconds if necessary. Stir until totally smooth, then dip the caramel portion of each pretzel rod into the chocolate, using a spoon to completely cover caramel. Place on parchment paper, then decorate while warm with candy sprinkles. Cool completely and enjoy.

Tiger Tails

PREP TIME: 15 MINUTES | COOK TIME: 5 MINUTES | YIELD: 6 PIECES

"You should also know that everyone runs from Shere Khan," the menacing tiger says to Mowgli with a flick of his tail.

These Tiger Tails, inspired by the fearsome beast, are toasted marshmallows dipped in chocolate and graham cracker crumbs in a fun twist on s'mores—no campfire required.

8 full graham cracker sheets

Nonstick cooking spray

18 marshmallows

2 cups milk chocolate chips

6 bamboo skewers

In the bowl of a food processor, break the graham crackers into small pieces. Blend until fine crumbs form.

Line the baking tray of a toaster oven with aluminum foil, then spray the foil with cooking spray. Place the marshmallows on the tray, spaced at least 1 inch apart. Set the toaster oven to "toast" and toast the marshmallows two to three cycles depending on toaster oven, until light golden brown. (Alternately, you can broil the marshmallows in the oven for 2 to 3 minutes.) The idea is to brown them slightly while retaining marshmallow shape. Remove and let the marshmallows cool.

Place the chocolate in a medium mixing bowl. Microwave for 45 seconds, then stir and microwave another 45 seconds. Stir until smooth.

Spear three marshmallows on each wooden skewer. Dip the marshmallows in chocolate, then immediately roll in graham cracker crumbs. Place coated marshmallow kebabs on a baking tray lined with parchment paper.

Using a spoon, drizzle some of the remaining chocolate on the graham cracker crumbs in tiger-stripe patterns. Chill in the refrigerator for 1 hour to set.

Evil Cream Horns

PREP TIME: 40 MINUTES | COOK TIME: 20 MINUTES | YIELD: 12 PIECES

Maleficent, the mistress of all evil, creates chaos and terror with powerful spells and curses. Aside from her pet raven at her side and flowing robes that cast a menacing silhouette, Maleficent is most recognizable by the dark twisted horns on her head. These cream horns have a diabolical twist: They have purple blackberry cream inside and black sugar outside, evoking Maleficent's iconic look.

Nonstick cooking spray

2 sheets puff pastry, thawed

1 egg, beaten with 1 tablespoon water (for egg wash to brush on pastry)

4 tablespoons (or more) black decorating sugar

2 teaspoons plain gelatin

3 scant tablespoons water

2 cups heavy cream

½ cup confectioners sugar

2 tablespoons seedless blackberry preserves

1 teaspoon vanilla extract

Purple gel paste (optional)

12 blackberries, for garnish

Prepare the cones. Fold a 12-inch sheet of aluminum foil n half (6-inch square) then roll into a cone shape. Repeat to make 12 cones. You can also use bakers' pastry cone molds. Spray each with cooking spray.

Unfold thawed puff pastry, and cut each sheet lengthwise into six equal strips. Gently stretch a pastry strip until it's a few inches longer and more pliable. Wrap pastry around a cone, overlapping to prevent gaps in pastry cones; press to adhere dough to ensure attachment during baking. Seal final edge with egg wash. Repeat with the remaining dough. Place pastry horns, seam sides down, on a baking sheet lined with parchment paper, allowing space between each.

Preheat oven to 400°F. Brush exposed dough (not the pastry touching paper) with egg wash then sprinkle generously with the black sugar. Place the bowl of a stand mixer in the freezer to chill.

Bake for 20 minutes, until golden brown. Remove from oven. Cool pastry on the shaped cones.

Prepare the cream. In a small heatproof bowl, combine the gelatin and water. Let stand for 5 minutes. Microwave for 10 seconds to liquefy the gelatin; whisk until smooth.

In the chilled mixer bowl, combine the cream, sugar, preserves, and vanilla. Whip the cream on medium-high, slowly drizzling gelatin into the bowl. Whip just until stiff peaks form. If desired, stir in a little purple gel to enhance color of pastry cream. Chill until ready to use.

Just before serving, transfer the cream to a pastry bag fitted with a large star tip. Generously fill each horn, then garnish with a blackberry. Serve immediately (filled cream horns quickly become soggy.)

Drinks

Peddler's Disguise

Anastasia & Drizella

Shiny Tai

Painting the Frozé Red

Peddler's Disguise

PREP TIME: 5 MINUTES | COOK TIME: 10 MINUTES | YIELD: 6 SERVINGS

When the Evil Queen discovers that Snow White is still alive, she immediately heads to her dungeon laboratory to devise a potion that will change her appearance and allow her to get to the girl undetected. "Now, a formula to transform my beauty into ugliness, change my queenly raiment to a peddler's cloak," she says. "Mummy dust, to make me old. To shroud my clothes, the black of night. To age my voice, an old hag's cackle. To whiten my hair, a scream of fright! A blast of wind to fan my hate. A thunderbolt to mix it well." The result of the queen's magic spell is Peddler's Disguise, a potion that masks her identity as an old peddler woman and allows her to give Snow White the poison apple that puts her to sleep.

This concoction won't turn you into anyone else, but it does make the house smell so good that you might think it's magic. Adults can add 1 ounce of dark or spiced rum per serving after cooking to make it a spiked beverage.

8 cups fresh apple cider or unfiltered apple juice

2 cinnamon sticks

1 orange, sliced into thin wheels

4 whole cloves

1-inch piece of fresh ginger

In a large saucepan over medium heat, combine all the ingredients. Bring to a simmer for 5 minutes.

Ladle into mugs, avoiding the solids in the pan. Garnish with the orange slices, if desired. Enjoy warm.

Anastasia & Drizella

PREP TIME: 5 MINUTES | YIELD: 2 SERVINGS

Evil stepsisters Anastasia and Drizella tear apart Cinderella's dress before they head off to the ball at the palace. While their dresses weren't made by birds and mice, they are vivid, eye-catching frocks: one pink, and one green. These bright color mocktails evoke the stepsisters' personalities— they're brightly colored, and because they're low in sugar, not very sweet. (Adults could add 2 ounces of gin or vodka for a refreshing summer cocktail.)

FOR THE SIMPLE SYRUP

½ cup granulated sugar

½ cup water

ANASTASIA

2 orange wedges, plus more
    for garnish

3 strawberries

1 ounce simple syrup

Club soda

DRIZELLA

1 lemon wedge, plus more
    for garnish

2 slices kiwi, peeled

4 blueberries

1 ounce simple syrup

Club soda

Prepare the simple syrup. In a small sauce pan, combine the sugar and water and bring to a boil, stirring to completely dissolve sugar. Remove from heat, and allow to cool.

For either cocktail, squeeze citrus fruit into a pint glass to release the juice. Add the fruit and simple syrup from the same recipe. Muddle with a spoon or a muddler until fruit is mostly broken down. (If you prefer a drink without fruit bits, muddle in a pint glass then use a fine-mesh strainer to pour the juice into another glass, leaving pulp behind.)

Fill the glass with ice, then fill to the top with club soda. Stir to mix, and garnish with a citrus wedge.

Shiny Tai

PREP TIME: 5 MINUTES | YIELD: 1 SERVING

"I'll never hide. I can't, I'm too shiny," Tamatoa sings as he attempts to trap Moana and Maui in his underwater lair. "Watch me dazzle like a diamond in the rough. Strut my stuff. My stuff is so shiny."

This Shiny Tai is a nonalcoholic version of a Mai Tai, a fruity drink brings forth the feeling of sailing the seven seas. Edible glitter makes the ice cubes shiny, and the juices will make you feel like you're on vacation, just for a minute.

2 ounces pineapple juice

2 ounces orange juice

Juice of 1 lime

½ ounce orgeat (almond syrup)

Crushed ice

2 sprigs fresh mint, for garnish

In a shaker, combine all the juices and the syrup with ice. Shake until chilled.

Strain into a rocks glass filled with crushed ice.

Clap the fresh mint between your hands two or three times to release the fragrant oils. Garnish and serve.

Painting the Frozé Red

PREP TIME: 5 MINUTES | YIELD: 2 SERVINGS

When they accidentally plant white roses rather than red, the Card Soldiers try to fix the problem before the Queen of Hearts notices. "She'd raise a fuss and each of us would quickly lose his head," they sing. "Since this is the part we dread, we're painting the roses red."

This nonalcoholic riff on Frozé uses fresh fruit and fruit juices to recreate the feeling of the wine-based cocktail without spirits. (Adults: If you substitute Rosé and a splash of vodka for the lemonade, you won't be disappointed.)

1 cup frozen strawberries

1 cup strawberry lemonade

Juice of 1 orange

1 teaspoon grenadine

1 cup ice

1 fresh strawberries, halved

In a blender, combine all ingredients. Blend until smooth. Divide between 2 glasses. Garnish with strawberry halves.

NUTRITIOUS TIP: Strawberries are a terrific source of antioxidants, as well as vital nutrients such as manganese and potassium.

Index

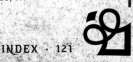

About the Author

Julie Tremaine is a food and travel writer who has written about theme parks for *Travel + Leisure*, *CNN Travel*, *Forbes*, *The Takeout*, and *Glamour*, and she's the Disneyland editor for *SFGate*. Julie is the author of *Supernatural: The Official Cookbook*, recipe contributor for *The Office: The Official Party Planning Guide to Planning Parties*, and co-author of *Life with the Afterlife: 13 Truths I've Learned about Ghosts* with paranormal researcher Amy Bruni. When she's not in Los Angeles, California, or Providence, Rhode Island, you'll likely find her at Epcot, tasting her way around the World Showcase. Read Julie's work at Travel-Sip-Repeat.com.

Acknowledgments

I wrote and cooked for this book all across the country, and couldn't have made it work without my mom, Beth-Anne Tremaine, who was always ready, cake spatula in hand, to help. Thanks to cookbook author Paul Feinstein and Disney writer and podcaster Kristen Carr for their endlessly creative suggestions, Buddy and Ginny Tremaine for giving over their kitchen to the madness of recipe testing, Jilly Gagnon and Danny O'Neill for the wine pairings, and my friends at the Fountain Avenue Collective for their eager appetites and honest feedback. Together, we've made something wickedly delicious.

INSIGHT EDITIONS

PO Box 3088
San Rafael, CA 94912
www.insighteditions.com

f Find us on Facebook: www.facebook.com/InsightEditions
🐦 Follow us on Twitter: @insighteditions

𝒟𝒾𝓈𝓃𝑒𝓎

Library of Congress Cataloging-in-Publication Data available.

ISBN: 978-1-64722-374-8

INSIGHT EDITIONS
Publisher: Raoul Goff
VP of Licensing and Partnerships: Vanessa Lopez
VP of Creative: Chrissy Kwasnik
VP of Manufacturing: Alix Nicholaeff
Editorial Director: Vicki Jaeger
Designer: Judy Wiatrek Trum
Editor: Maya Alpert
Production Editor: Jennifer Bentham
Production Manager: Eden Orlesky
Senior Production Manager, Subsidiary Rights: Lina S. Palma

WATERBURY PUBLICATIONS, INC.
Editorial Director: Lisa Kingsley
Creative Director: Ken Carlson
Associate Editor: Tricia Bergman
Associate Editor: Maggie Glisan
Associate Art Director: Doug Samuelson
Production Assistant: Mindy Samuelson
Photographer: Ken Carlson
Food Stylist: Jennifer Peterson
Food Stylist Assistant: Catherine Fitzpatrick

Insight Editions, in association with Roots of Peace, will plant two trees for each tree used in the manufacturing of this book. Roots of Peace is an internationally renowned humanitarian organization dedicated to eradicating land mines worldwide and converting war-torn lands into productive farms and wildlife habitats. Roots of Peace will plant two million fruit and nut trees in Afghanistan and provide farmers there with the skills and support necessary for sustainable land use.

Manufactured in China by Insight Editions

10 9 8 7 6 5 4